Collins · do

Eight We

KS3

im Sweetman

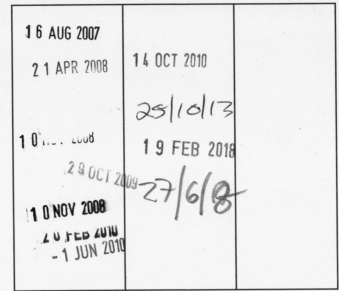

William Collins' dream of knowledge for all began with the publication of his first book in 1819. A self-educated mill worker, he not only enriched millions of lives, but also founded a flourishing publishing house. Today, staying true to this spirit, Collins books are packed with inspiration, innovation and practical expertise. They place you at the centre of a world of possibility and give you exactly what you need to explore it.

Collins. Do more.

Published by Collins
An imprint of HarperCollins*Publishers*
77 – 85 Fulham Palace Road
Hammersmith
London
W6 8JB

Browse the complete Collins catalogue at
www.collinseducation.com

© HarperCollins*Publishers* Limited 2005

10 9 8 7 6 5 4 3

ISBN-13 978 0 00 719929 7
ISBN-10 0 00 719929 5

Jim Sweetman asserts his moral right to be identified as the author of this work

British Library Cataloguing in Publication Data
A Catalogue record for this publication is available from the British Library

Written by Jim Sweetman
Edited by Philippa Boxer and Joanne Hunt
Design by Celia Hart and Chi Leung
Illustrations by Harriet Buckley, Fliss Cary, Celia Hart, Sarah Wimperis
Printed and bound in Hong Kong by Printing Express Ltd

You might also like to visit
www.harpercollins.co.uk
The book lover's website

Acknowledgements
The Publishers gratefully acknowledge the following for permission to reproduce copyright material:
Extracts from U S Department of Energy website (Office of Energy Efficiency and Renewable Energy).
www.eere.energy.gov. Reprinted with permission of U. S. Dept of Energy.
Greenpeace letter dated 25th August, 2004.
www.greenpeace.org.uk. Reprinted with permission.
Extracts from *No Horizon Is So Far* by Ann Bancroft, Liv Arnesen, and Cheryl Dahle, published by Perseus Publishing 2004.
'Invasion of Westminster' by Philip Webster, in *The Times*, 16th September, 2004. © The Times, London 2004. Reprinted with permission.
Extract from *Angus, Thongs and Full-Frontal Snogging: Confessions of Georgia Nicholson* by Louise Rennison, published by Piccadilly Press, 1999. © Louise Rennison 1999. Reprinted with permission of Piccadilly Press.
Extract from *On The Bright Side, I'm Now The Girlfriend Of A Sex God: Further, Further Confessions of Georgia Nicholson*, published by Piccadilly Press. © Louise Rennison. Reprinted with permission of Piccadilly Press.
Figures relating to Natural Disasters belong to the ISDR.
'Bored' by Margaret Atwood, from *The Atlantic Monthly*: December 1994. Volume 272, No 6 pg 102. © Margaret Atwood.

Extract from *Across the Plains in the Donner Party* by Virginia Reed Murphy, edited by Karen Zeinert, published by Shoe String Press 1985. Reprinted with the kind permission of Mr. J. Zeinert.
Extract from *Holes* by Louis Sachar, published by Bloomsbury. Reprinted with permission of Bloomsbury.
2 short extracts taken from *The Metro*, 20 October 2004. Reprinted by permission of Solo Syndications.
Extract from http://4hydrogen.com written by Captain Ozone. Reprinted with the kind permission of the site.
Photographs
p27 Animal Aid
p35 Greenpeace windfarm photograph. Reprinted with permission of Greenpeace UK.
p51 © Reuters/CORBIS
p69 © Russell Boyce/Reuters/CORBIS
p77 Robinsons Soft Drinks Ltd
p86 Hydrogen bus picture used courtesy of the FCIA Pty Limited.

Whilst every effort has been made to trace the copyright holders, in cases where this has been unsuccessful, or if any have inadvertently been overlooked, the Publishers will be pleased to make the necessary arrangements at the first opportunity.

CONTENTS

INTRODUCTION

Does this sound like you?

You know you should have started earlier but you haven't. The National Tests are just a few weeks away and you haven't even thought about revising because you thought you had ages. Or is it because you hate the whole revision thing – hours of staring at dull text books and badly taken class notes? Well don't despair, help is at hand in the form of *Eight Weeks Flat KS3 English*.

Why Eight Weeks Flat?

This colourful, easy-to-follow revision guide will help you prepare for those important Tests. The book covers material at levels 4, 5 and 6 and is mainly designed for students hoping to gain a level 5 or 6 in English at Key Stage 3.

Eight Weeks Flat KS3 English follows a week-by-week, day-by-day plan to help you break down your revision into small chunks. The plan is designed to spread your revision out into 40 sessions to be completed over eight weeks. However, if you started a bit earlier, you can give yourself an occasional day off or use the time to redo a skill you are not so sure about. If you have not left enough time, aim to do two skills a day.

How Eight Weeks Flat works

Each weekday you tackle a different skill. Each revision session consists of a page of important subject content and a page of follow-up practice activities. Start by reading all the notes and examples. The activity questions include some short tasks and some extended writing ones. Attempt them all, as it is only through practising your skills that you will see any improvement. You could set yourself a time limit in order to motivate you and promise yourself a treat when you've finished.

Detailed answers and advice on how to mark the questions are provided at the back of the book (see page 94). Mark your work as you finish revising each skill so that you can spot any weaker areas. You need to be your own worst critic in English if you are really to see a great improvement in your writing.

After you have completed all 40 revision sessions, have a go at the Practice test (see page 85). This test is split into the Reading, Writing and Shakespeare papers and includes both longer and shorter tasks. Remember that spelling is also assessed (as part of the shorter task in the Writing paper).

Ask someone to mark your Practice test or do it yourself. Add up your marks and use the level tables (see page 96) to help decide the level you achieved. Remember – this is just an indication of your actual level.

If you have worked your way through the book and still have some time left for revision, go back and have another go at some of the sessions you didn't do so well the first time.

Best of luck!

About the National Tests

Just in case you are not sure how it all works, here is some information about the actual Tests.

At the beginning of May in Year 9 you will sit National Tests in English (as well as in Maths and Science). For English you will take three Tests altogether:

Writing	Longer task	: 30 marks	45 minutes
	Shorter task	: 20 marks	30 minutes
Reading	3 extracts	: 32 marks	1 hour 15 minutes
Shakespeare	2 scenes	: 18 marks	45 minutes

The Writing paper is 1 hour and 15 minutes long and consists of a longer and a shorter writing task. You have 45 minutes for the longer writing task which includes 15 minutes of recommended planning time.

The completed Tests are sent away to be marked. You should find out how you have done early in July. You should be aiming for at least a level 5 or 6 in your English Test.

STORY BASICS: ELEMENTS OF TEXTS

What you need to know

1 Recognise the difference between fiction and non-fiction texts.

2 Understand the meaning of key words for talking about texts.

3 Know how to use these terms in your writing.

FICTION OR NON-FICTION?

- **Fiction** refers to any text that is about something 'made up'. It is 'make believe'. All stories are works of fiction.

- **Non-fiction** texts are any texts that refer to real or true things, e.g. newspaper articles, leaflets, brochures and information-based websites.

- With non-fiction texts, you need to work out the text's purpose. Is it to inform, explain or describe, or to argue, advise or persuade?

TALKING TERMS

- You need to be familiar with the terms used to describe texts.

- **Setting**: the place and time in which the story takes place. The place could be real or made-up. The time can be in the present, the past or the future.

- **Atmosphere**: the way the setting 'feels'. It may be dark and sinister (as in *Macbeth*, for example), or it could be light and positive and magical.

- **Mood/tone**: similar to **atmosphere** but it refers to the 'feeling' of the whole text, not just the setting. It refers to the language that the writer has used: is it dark or depressing or joyful?

- **Plot**: the storyline that runs through the text, i.e. what actually *happens*.

- **Language**: the words that the writer uses or the way in which he/she puts the message across.

- **Imagery**: figures of speech which the writer uses to create a 'picture' in the reader's mind. Examples are **metaphors** (when the writer says that something *is* something else) and **similes** (when the writer says something *is like* something else).

- **Theme**: the ideas that run through a text, e.g. love, fear, death or power. Each text will have its own themes that it discusses or illustrates.

- **Character**: the individual people who appear in a text.

- **Characterisation**: the way in which the writer puts a character across or the process of creating a character in writing.

- **Narrative voice**: the person in the text who is telling the story. This can be in the first person (I) or in the third person (he/she).

STORY BASICS: ELEMENTS OF TEXTS

1 Read the following introduction to a story. Then complete the questions below.

The house was surrounded by thick, dark hedges and could hardly be seen, but passers by on the road outside sometimes caught a glimpse of light in its attic windows or heard strange sounds echoing from the broken door. I had heard so many stories about this house and on one evening that was to change my life forever, I decided that I wanted to find out the truth.

Crouching down so as not to be seen under the flickering lights of the street-lamp, with rain lashing about my face and my new jeans soaked through to the skin, I peeped through a tiny gap in the dense hedge. Through the twisted branches and thorny undergrowth I gasped as I saw in the shadows a figure – cloaked in black and taller than a man but stooped like a giant ape.

The figure turned and began looking about urgently.

"Jamie, you big idiot!" I said to myself but then realised that I had disturbed him and that he was trying to work out where the little sound had come from. I held my breath and felt my whole body tense up, my jaw locking, heart nearly missing a beat, but I knew that it was too late. I knew that he had seen me, as with an ugly roar he came charging towards the hedge with his arms flailing and his eyes wide and wild.

(a) This text is written using third person narration. True or false?

_____

(b) Describe the setting.

_____

_____

(c) Describe the atmosphere.

_____

_____

_____

(d) Who is narrating the story and how do we know this?

_____

_____

(e) What is the mood or tone of the text? How does the language show this? Give **two** examples.

_____

_____

(f) Find an example of a simile in the text.

_____

_____

STORY BASICS: CHARACTERS AND DESCRIPTIONS

What you need to know

1. Understand what characters add to a story.
2. Appreciate the need for strong description.

CHARACTERS

- All stories rely on **characters** to make them interesting or exciting. Good writers invent characters that the reader is able to relate to and 'get to know'.

DESCRIPTION

- Using **description** in characterisation creates strong characters.

> Jamie appeared at Nan's door. Jamie is small and poor and not very happy.

> Nan heard the door creak open very hesitantly and there in the doorframe, head bowed forlornly, with his hair unbrushed, eyes cast down towards his battered trainers, one foot placed nervously atop the other, stood the little dishevelled figure of Jamie.

- The second description of Jamie is much more vivid and effective than the first. We need to look at *why*.
- The first does not describe how Jamie looks or the way he is behaving, it merely states the facts. Weak writers simply *tell* the reader the bare facts, whereas a stronger writer will *show* the audience – rather like presenting an image before their eyes. That way, the audience builds up the 'fact-file' about the character themselves.
- Descriptions can be enriched using:
  - **adjectives** which describe a noun (object/person), e.g. '**battered** trainers';
  - **adverbs**, which describe a verb (doing word) e.g. 'one foot placed **nervously** atop the other'.

<u>Remember</u>
The *way* a character does something can show the reader an awful lot. We don't just want to hear what happens, but how. It is only when you show *how*, that there is an effect on the reader. If the reader is not affected he/she will not read the text!

STORY BASICS: CHARACTERS AND DESCRIPTIONS

1 You are going to create your own character in the same sort of way that Jamie was created.

(a) Begin by gathering information about your character and get to know him/her yourself. Fill in the 'Detail' column of the chart below. Most of the words that you use will be **adjectives**. Then add actions and mannerisms that would *show* that your character is like this.

Feature	Detail (adjectives)	How could the character show this?
name	Jane	
age	16	
appearance	really	
manner		
attitude	good	
mood		
fears		
hopes		

(b) Now put all of this together into a paragraph. Make your writing as interesting and professional as you can. Try hard to create a picture in the reader's mind.

STORY BASICS: USING TENSION

What you need to know

1 Understand how and why writers build tension.

2 Appreciate the effect that tension has on the reader.

TENSION

- **Tension** is when the reader is 'on the edge of his/her seat', reading quickly.
- A writer can create tension in a number of ways:
  - play with the pace and the rhythm of the text, using punctuation to speed up or slow down the text;
  - use a lot of description to conjure up a tense atmosphere;
  - 'tease' the reader by giving more and more detail but postpone the 'event' to keep the reader hanging on.

CLIMAX AND ANTI-CLIMAX

- The **highest point of tension** or the point that the tension builds up to is called the **climax**. If the tension is released and there is no climax, this is called an **anti-climax**.
- Here is an example from Charles Dickens' *Great Expectations*.

At such a time I found out for certain, that this bleak place overgrown with nettles was the churchyard…and that the dark flat wilderness beyond the churchyard, intersected with dykes and mounds and gates, with scattered cattle feeding on it, was the marshes; that the low leaden line beyond, was the river; and that the distant savage lair from which the wind was rushing, was the sea; and that the small bundle of shivers growing afraid of it all and beginning to cry, was Pip.

"Hold your noise!" cried a terrible voice, as a man started up from among the graves at the side of the church porch. "Keep still, you little devil, or I'll cut your throat!"

A fearful man, all in coarse grey, with a great iron on his leg. A man with no hat, and with broken shoes, and with an old rag tied round his head. A man who had been soaked in water, and smothered in mud, and lamed by stones, and cut by flints, and stung by nettles, and torn by briars; who limped, and shivered, and glared and growled; and whose teeth chattered in his head as he seized me by the chin.

STORY BASICS: USING TENSION

1 Create a short piece in which you build up tension in your writing.

Use the techniques you have looked at to build up tension in your writing. You may wish to refer back to page 6 (**Week 1, Monday**) for another example of tension in writing. Remember to use paragraphs correctly.

Base your work on the following stimulus:

> You are in bed, at home alone; you hear a noise from downstairs; you make the journey downstairs; you realise the noise is coming from behind the kitchen door; you push open the door.

End the piece with what you find behind the door – this can either be a climax or a release of tension, it is up to you.

PUNCTUATION: PARAGRAPHS

What you need to know

1. Know how to organise your ideas into paragraphs.
2. Know when you need to start a new paragraph.

WHAT ARE PARAGRAPHS FOR?

- Each **paragraph** in a piece of writing contains linked information, themes or ideas. Breaking up your ideas in this way is the *only* effective way of organising your writing.
- Paragraphs help your reader to follow your ideas. Your writing will flow and seem logical and intelligent.

WHEN DO I USE A NEW PARAGRAPH?

- The **introduction** should be one, clear paragraph, as should the **conclusion**.
- You begin a new paragraph when there is a *change* of:

  - time   - place   - action   - idea   - character

"Jamie, you big idiot!" I said to myself but then realised that I had disturbed him and that he was trying to work out where the little sound had come from. I held my breath and felt my whole body tense up, my jaw locking, heart nearly missing a beat, but I knew that it was too late. I knew that he had seen me, as with an ugly roar he came charging towards the hedge with his arms flailing and his eyes wide and wild.

Where my body had been frozen and rigid, it suddenly leapt into life like a cheetah. I sprang to my feet and ran as fast as my legs were able to take me, heart pounding, lungs on fire, without once looking back.

- In the example above, the writer has begun another paragraph when Jamie runs away from the scary scene. This is because there has been a **change of action**.

PUNCTUATION: PARAGRAPHS

1 Look at paragraphs **A – D** below. Write down the order you think they should be written and state why.

A When the writer moves on to discuss a new idea, it is important that he/she begins a new paragraph. This prevents ideas from becoming confused and the power of the meaning being lost.

B The concluding paragraph is also very important, as this is what the reader reads last – and it often plays an important role in how they will remember your work. You need to make sure that this last paragraph is strong, has a definite purpose and rounds off your work.

C Any piece of continuous writing needs to be organised into sensible and logical paragraphs. There are certain rules that a writer must follow to ensure that his/her writing flows logically.

D When you have finished writing an essay or a story, you should always make sure that you look back and read through what you have written to check for accurate paragraph breaks. Remember it is not just after a new idea, but a new time, action or character will also require a new paragraph.

_____

_____

_____

_____

_____

_____

_____

2 Write a description of your local area to go onto a website. Use **three** separate paragraphs to describe where you live, the surroundings and the community.

_____

_____

_____

_____

_____

_____

_____

_____

_____

_____

_____

_____

WRITING: PLANNING

What you need to know

1 Understand that planning is the first stage of the writing process.

2 Know that using a plan will improve your writing.

HOW TO START PLANNING

- One way to get your ideas onto paper is to draw a spider diagram. This helps you to see your ideas before you decide on an order for them. Start with the central idea in the middle, and branch out from there as new ideas come to you.

  If you had been asked to comment on a character in a play, your spider diagram may look something like this:

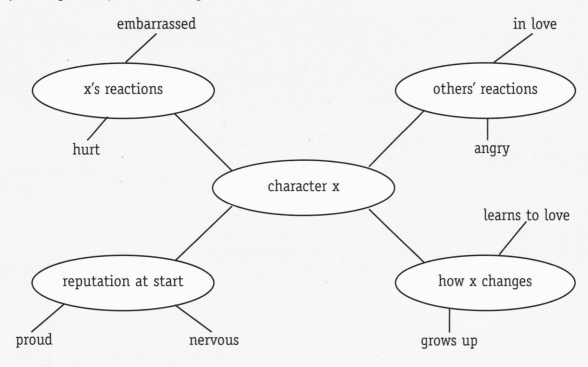

SORTING YOUR IDEAS AND ORDERING INTO PARAGRAPHS

- Your spider diagram may seem like one big jumble, with lots of ideas all over the place. You will need to group similar ideas together. You can do this by using several different coloured pens and by marking similar ideas in the same colour.

- When your ideas are in colour-coded groups, write them in separate lists. You will find that each group forms a paragraph – or can be broken down into several.

- Decide what information will go into which paragraph. Then decide on a heading for each paragraph to ensure that the purpose of each one is clear. (Do not include headings in your finished piece though – it is very bad style!)

  For help with the rules of paragraphing look back to page 11.

- Now decide on a logical order for your paragraphs and number each one. Think about the order carefully – a sensible and logical order will make your ideas flow and your argument intelligent.

- Once you have your ideas organised into a logical order, make sure that you know what you are going to say in each paragraph before you start.

1 Make a plan for a piece of writing about yourself and your life. In the space below, make notes, in the form of a spider diagram. You may wish to consider the following: your early childhood, your family, starting school, pets, happy memories, likes and dislikes, friends.

2 Using several different coloured pens, mark the ideas that you think belong together in the same colour.

3 Write out the content of each group in the space below. Then decide on a short heading for each one. You may need to break some down into shorter paragraphs.

4 Decide on an order by numbering each paragraph.

READING: RETRIEVING KEY WORDS

What you need to know

1 Understand how to get the most from your reading of a text.

2 Understand how to retrieve the information you need.

WHAT IS THE BEST WAY TO READ A TEXT?

- The main way to improve your reading is to practise reading and summarising texts. The more you read, the easier you will find it is to **retrieve** information from a text.

- Following the steps below will help to make your reading more effective.

  1 Start by reading a text right through. Do not stop at anything you do not understand – you can come back to it. Read it through to get a 'feel' for the style and the content of the text.

  2 Read through the text again and underline the key words in each paragraph. Underline the **topic sentence** in each paragraph.

  3 Now go through the text again, this time making a note beside each paragraph to **summarise** its content. You should not write more than a few words. This will help you to have an overview.

  4 Finally, you may wish to go back and read it again, this time looking up any words or terms that you do not understand in a dictionary.

- Try this technique as often as you can, even when reading newspapers and magazines. Your reading *will* improve – that is guaranteed.

'Now, what is this paragraph actually saying?'

ANSWERING READING QUESTIONS

- When you are asked specific questions on a text, you need to be able to go to the right part of the text. Having a clear understanding of the key words will help you to do this. It is helpful to have both a dictionary and a thesaurus at hand when practising reading activities.

- Make sure that you know exactly what the question is asking you to find. The more familiar you are with the article, the easier it will be to go to the right part of the text and to retrieve the relevant information.

READING: RETRIEVING KEY WORDS

1 Read the following extract and answer the questions below.

> I travelled to see this so-called monstrosity for myself. From close-up, the turbine is an elegant construction as it stands firm against the breeze with its curvaceous blades spinning with only the slightest whirr.

(a) What does the author of this text mean by the phrase 'so-called monstrosity'?

_____

_____

(b) What single word is used to describe the sound of the wind turbine?

_____

(c) Find **two** adjectives which show how the writer feels about the construction.

_____

_____

2 Read the following extract and answer the questions below.

> Using the wind to provide energy is not a recent discovery. Wind power was used to propel boats along the Nile River, in what we now know as Egypt, seven thousand years ago. In China, primitive wind pumps were used to pump water long before their use became famous in the Netherlands. The first windmills to grind grain were probably built in England over a thousand years ago. In the USA and Australia windmills were used by the first settlers to pump underground water to the surface and later to generate electricity for isolated dwellings.

(a) List **four** verbs (doing words) to show some of the different uses for wind power.

_____

(b) Find **three** words that could be replaced with the words *push, simple* and *lonely*.

_____

(c) When were the Ancient Egyptians using wind power?

_____

(d) Explain the meaning of the word 'dwellings'.

_____

_____

WRITING: TO INFORM

What you need to know

1. Identify the features of informative writing.
2. Use the features of information texts in your own writing.

WHAT ARE INFORMATION TEXTS?

- **Informational writing** gives you **facts**. It is a simple form of writing used to inform the reader.

- Information texts describe things as they are. They can describe a range of social, cultural or natural phenomena.

- Information texts are therefore **factual** texts. They are not trying to convince or persuade the reader of anything.

- Information texts do not use emotive language or heavy description, and are **impersonal**, unless they are about a personal topic.

  Information texts:
  - are written in the present tense;
  - use technical terms;
  - avoid the personal pronoun 'I' (unless it is a personal text);
  - introduce general information about the topic;
  - explain/describe the topic in detail, giving more specific information;
  - may use rhetorical questions to engage the reader's interest;
  - summarise in a conclusion.

- Information texts vary according to their purpose. A text that is providing tourist information on a tourist attraction, stately home or area of natural beauty will include a lot more description than a text that is reporting on scientific phenomena.

  Examples of information texts:
  - history books;
  - guide books;
  - factual reports;
  - academic research;
  - leaflets;
  - scientific journals;
  - travel writing.

Bury St Edmunds is a historic market town in Suffolk with a population of over 50 000 people. The town initially grew around an important abbey and developed into a flourishing clothmaking town by the 14th century. The abbey was largely destroyed during the 16th century but today Bury is known for its brewery, for flower displays each summer and for its attractive old town centre.

Wind is a form of solar energy. Winds are caused by the uneven heating of the atmosphere by the sun, the irregularities of the earth's surface, and rotation of the earth. Wind flow patterns are modified by the earth's terrain, bodies of water, and vegetation. Humans use this wind flow, or motion energy, for many purposes: sailing, flying a kite, and even generating electricity.

The terms 'wind energy' or 'wind power' describe the process by which the wind is used to generate mechanical power or electricity. Wind turbines convert the kinetic energy in the wind into mechanical power. This mechanical power can be used for specific tasks such as grinding grain or pumping water.

1 Select **three** phrases which tell you that the above is an informational text. For each one, give a reason why it tells you this.

(i) _____

_____

_____

(ii) _____

_____

_____

(iii) _____

_____

_____

2 Write your own informational text on any topic you know a lot about. Use **three** facts as the basis for **three** paragraphs, begin with an introduction and end with a summarising conclusion. Continue on an extra piece of paper if you need to.

_____

_____

_____

_____

_____

_____

_____

_____

_____

_____

_____

What you need to know

1 Recognise the features of plays.

2 Understand terms for talking about plays.

3 Appreciate the importance of the audience.

THE PURPOSE OF A PLAY

- A play is written to be performed on stage for an **audience** to watch. You must never forget that the words are intended to be *heard* and the characters are meant to be *seen*.

- When you read a scene, consider the following:

Who is on the stage and where is the scene set?

Make sure that you know which characters are present in this scene. Entrances and exits are written in the playscript. The setting will normally be given as a stage direction, but also the characters may give hints as to their surroundings, as King Duncan does here in the Shakespeare play, *Macbeth*.

> "This castle hath a pleasant seat; the air
> Nimbly and sweetly recommends itself
> Unto our gentle senses."

How does the stage actually *look*?

Picture in your mind exactly how the stage would be set up – where would the characters be standing and what would they be doing? Drawing a plan – or stage map – will help you to visualise this.

What do the characters know and what does the audience know?

Dramatic irony means that the audience knows something that the characters do not. It puts the audience in an interesting position.

How would the characters actually perform their lines?
How would the characters be portrayed?

You need to remember that every play has a director and that every actor will go about their presentation of a character differently. How do *you* think a character would best be put across to the audience? How would *you* direct the actor playing a certain part?

'Mmm that's how I would do it!'

READING: PLAYS

1 Take any scene from the Shakespeare play that you are studying. Read the scene through thoroughly and take time as you do so to *visualise* the scene in your own mind. Answer the following questions on the scene:

(a) Who is on stage? Do any characters enter/exit during the scene?

_____

_____

_____

(b) Where is the scene set?

_____

_____

_____

(c) What is happening?

_____

_____

_____

(d) How does the scene fit into the whole play? What is the purpose of this specific scene?

_____

_____

_____

(e) What theme(s) are illustrated here? (See **Week 1, Monday** for a definition of 'theme'.)

_____

_____

_____

(f) What is happening between the characters?

_____

_____

_____

(g) How is this shown to us visually?

_____

_____

_____

(h) How is this shown to us in the language?

_____

_____

_____

What you need to know

1. Understand a range of poetic terms.
2. Appreciate poetic effects.
3. Recognise the rhyme scheme of a poem.

POETIC FORM

- **Poetry** is about using language to put feelings across – feelings that are hard to express in another way. The best way to respond to a poem is to read it several times aloud and make a note of *your* reactions.

POETIC TERMS

- **Alliteration** – a group of words in which the same sound is repeated, e.g. slithering snakes.
- **Couplets** – a series of two lines that rhyme.
- **Imagery** – figures of speech in language to create images/pictures in the reader's mind to evoke feelings/states of mind.
- **Metaphor** – imagery, saying that one thing is something else, such as 'all the world's a stage' and 'eyes are the windows to the soul'.

- **Narrator/narrative voice** – the voice/person who is 'saying' the poem.
- **Onomatopoeia** – imagery, when words are used to imitate/evoke sounds, such as crash, buzz, boom.
- **Personification** – imagery, when non-human objects or ideas are given human qualities.
- **Rhyme** – when two or more words end in the same sound.
- **Rhythm** – the beat of the poem.
- **Simile** – imagery, saying that something is like something else.
- **Stanza** – the 'poetry' term for 'verse'.
- **Tone** – the feeling created by the voice.

WORKING OUT THE RHYME SCHEME

- Call your first line A.
- If the next line rhymes with A call it A, otherwise call it B.
- If there is no rhyme, it will just go A,B,C,D,E... .
- Here is a simple rhyme:

There was a young student called Brad	A
Who thought he was a bit of a lad	A
He would stand up and shout	B
And ask all the girls out	B
But the others just thought he was sad.	A

1 Read the following poem, *Remember,* by Christina Georgina Rossetti, a Victorian poet.

> Remember me when I am gone away,
> Gone far away into the silent land;
> When you can no more hold me by the hand,
> Nor I half turn to go yet turning stay.
> Remember me when no more day by day
> You tell me of our future that you plann'd:
> Only remember me; you understand
> It will be late to counsel then or pray.
> Yet if you should forget me for a while
> And afterwards remember, do not grieve:
> For if the darkness and corruption leave
> A vestige of the thoughts that once I had,
> Better by far you should forget and smile
> Than that you should remember and be sad.

(a) Read through this poem (aloud if you can) and then decide what the rhyme scheme is.

_____

(b) What is the theme of this poem?

_____

(c) The poet uses the metaphor 'silent land'. What does she mean by this?

_____

(d) Who is the voice addressing? How do we know? Find a line from the poem to support your answer.

_____

_____

_____

_____

(e) Why does the poet say to the reader 'do not grieve'?

_____

_____

_____

_____

_____

What you need to know

1 Understand the difference between direct and reported speech.

2 Know how to use speech marks.

3 Recognise that using a range of alternatives to 'said' improves your writing.

DIRECT OR REPORTED SPEECH?

- You will need to be able to use both **direct** and **reported speech** in your writing. There is a big difference between these two methods of telling the reader about what someone has said.

- Direct speech is when you use *the actual words* that the person used. The rule is the same as for quoting any language: you *must* use **speech marks** to show that the text is not your own words.

- Reported speech is when you explain what the person said *in your own words*. You do not use speech marks and you have to make sure that you *report* the speech properly, so any references to 'I' are removed and are replaced with he/she.

- If you were to write about the conversation above using reported speech you would say:

Martin said that he could not believe what Lisa said to Jake last night.

- If you were to write about the conversation using direct speech you would say:

Simone replied by saying, "Didn't you hear what he said to her in English yesterday?" which shows that she is on Lisa's side.

- When you use direct speech, you must *always* make sure that each time you use a new speaker, you start a new line.

"Who did she think she was?" said Martin, accusingly.
"I know what you mean, Martin, but I think he deserved it," replied Simone.

PUNCTUATION: DIRECT AND REPORTED SPEECH

1 Change the sentences below from direct to reported speech.

(a) "What time is it?" asked Harry.

_____

(b) "Slow down, I can't hear a word you are saying," Miss Parker remarked.

_____

_____

2 Change the following sentences from reported speech to direct speech.

(a) The postman said that he was sick of the dog at number 42.

_____

_____

(b) Salma told Louise that she was going ice-skating that evening.

_____

_____

3 Write down as many interesting alternatives to the word 'said' as you can.

_____

_____

_____

4 Use direct speech to write the dialogue between two teenagers who are arguing about a £20 note they have just found on the floor outside a shop. Should they keep it, take it into the shop or tell the police? Use speech marks carefully.

_____

_____

_____

_____

_____

_____

_____

_____

_____

_____

_____

_____

_____

What you need to know

1 Understand how description can create pictures.

2 Recognise how personal references can enrich writing.

3 Build upon the basics in descriptive writing.

CHOOSING WORDS

- You have already looked at using **description** in your writing on page 7. In this section you are going to look at **word choice** and how you can create pictures and inspire your reader.

- Weak description is not interesting. The choice of adjective is very important. To make your writing interesting, tell your reader *more*. You want the reader to be able to *see* the image that is in your head or before your eyes. It is the job of the writer to make sure that the reader can do this.

- This does not mean that you need to describe something over and over. If you use strong, visual images, this will not be necessary.

- The text below is written by Ann Bancroft, one of the first two women to walk across Antarctica. You are almost able to share the view that she describes of the scene she is looking at.

That evening, we watched the high Antarctic sun dip slightly and the sky grow pink, a clear indication that winter was coming. The sun never sets during the summers, so the evening hour is a long flirtation between the sun and the horizon, like lovers who gaze at each other from across a room but never touch. Wisps of cloud turned violet and streaks of sapphire blue appeared behind the peaks of the white-capped mountains with giant glaciers suspended between them. Just beyond the black, rounded humps of the mountain called the Matador (for it looks like a bullfighter's cap) there was even a bit of red in the rocks. I would not have traded this sight of the Antarctic sky for a thousand Caribbean sunsets. For in Antarctica, there is nothing between you and the sky – no trees, no buildings, no poles, no electric lines. You can see for hundreds of kilometres along the horizon, where the sky meets the ice under your feet. It seems that the sky is not only above you, but also next to you and in front of you. You are walking into the sky as much as you are walking on the snow and ice.

(*No Horizon Is So Far* by Ann Bancroft, Liv Arnesen and Cheryl Dahle)

25

WRITING: LOOKING AGAIN AT DESCRIPTION

1 Read again the description by Ann Bancroft on page 25. Underline the parts of the text (sentences or particular words) where you feel the description is especially vivid.

2 Fill in the gaps in the following phrases to create your own vivid images. Remember, there are no rights and wrongs – just be creative with language and see what beautiful images you can create.

(a) _____ of smoke _____ through the air.

(b) Ice formed in _____ and created a _____

on the pavement.

(c) Leaves fell like _____ .

(d) The _____ danced like _____ through/off/on

the _____ of _____ .

(e) The cold chill felt like _____

_____ .

(f) _____ of rain left _____ across/on/in

the_____ of the _____ .

3 Write your own description of a place where you have been. It could be somewhere you have journeyed to only once, a place from a holiday or day out or a place from your neighbourhood – somewhere special to you. Try to capture the place and your feelings about it in the language you use.

_____

_____

_____

_____

_____

_____

_____

_____

_____

_____

_____

_____

_____

_____

WRITING: TO ARGUE

What you need to know

1. Know how argument differs from persuasion.
2. Know where to use argument.

HOW DO ARGUMENT AND PERSUASION DIFFER?

- **Persuasion** is sensible and rational and puts forward a case. **Argument** does this, too, but it also goes further.
- Argument writing is an angrier, more aggressive way of writing. It is more emotive and does not try to be subtle.

FEATURES OF ARGUMENT

- Moral imperatives and exclamations:

  Do not allow scientific experiments on animals!

- More emotional language:

  Animal experiments amount to exploitation and torture of innocent creatures. They are unnecessary, cruel and evil.

- Threats:

  More violent demonstrations will be held until you end the cruelty.

- Rhetorical questions (where the answer is obvious):

  How would you feel having hairspray squirted into your eyes until you go blind?

- 'Second guessing' (predict the counter-arguments or responses of the reader and then challenge and disprove them):

  There are many who would argue that animal testing is necessary to ensure that cosmetics are safe for human use. This argument is clearly an unfounded and concerning one, as it provokes the question: 'what on earth are cosmetic companies encouraging women to put on their skin that require such tests?'

1   Imagine that your local council is going to build a large motorway right through the area where you live. You are writing a letter to the Mayor against the proposal. Remember your aim is to stir people up, to make them agree with you.
Use emotive language, threats and rhetorical questions in your speech. Try to predict your reader's counter-arguments and then challenge them.

_____

_____

_____

_____

_____

_____

_____

_____

_____

_____

_____

_____

_____

_____

_____

_____

_____

_____

_____

_____

_____

_____

_____

_____

_____

_____

_____

_____

_____

PUNCTUATION: COMMAS

What you need to know

1 Know how and where to use commas in writing.

2 Know the function of the comma in lists.

WHERE TO USE THE COMMA

- The **comma** is one of the most useful punctuation marks. Being able to use it in the right places shows you are a competent writer. These are some of the places where you should use a comma:

  ■ To emphasise a pause in your writing.

  > She was always kind to her own pets, but could be nasty to other animals.

  ■ To separate parts of a sentence.

  > As he entered the room, she was immediately conscious of the stranger's presence.

  ■ To separate items in a list.

  > At the end of a match, he always feels tired, invigorated, happy and thirsty.

  ■ To show links between clauses in a sentence.

  > He noticed that the old lady, who had not spoken for some time, had now fallen asleep.

  ■ To mark direct speech.

  > "There is one thing," he said, "to remember above all others, and that is to treat others as you would have them treat you".

- There are no hard and fast rules about the use of the comma and too many can make your writing look untidy. Often, commas are most effective when used in pairs.

  The important thing is to think about whether a comma will help your writing to communicate more effectively to a reader.

PUNCTUATION: COMMAS

1 Put commas in the correct places in the following sentences. The number of commas per sentence is given in brackets.

(a) Mr Flash who was in the queue for the cash machine was held up at gunpoint. (2)

(b) Red white and blue are the colours of the Dutch flag. (1)

(c) After hours of preparation and many tears she was ready for the longest most challenging race of her career. (2)

2 Do the same activity with the following passages.

(a) This extract by Charles Dickens contains **ten** commas in the original!

> When he came to the low church wall he got over it like a man whose legs were numbed and stiff and then turned round to look for me. When I saw him turning I set my face towards home and made the best use of my legs. But presently I looked over my shoulder and saw him going on again towards the river still hugging himself in both arms and picking his way with his sore feet among the great stones dropped into the marshes here and there for stepping-places when the rains were heavy or the tide was in.

(b) This extract needs something other than just commas. Can you see what else is missing?

> At the start of the second half Woodhead Athletic began to dominate the match. Get forward more shouted the captain draw the defenders to the wings. Stuart pushed forward and then suddenly a dream ball from Cortez the young talented Argentinian centre-back arrived at his feet. One two three steps and Stuart hit the ball running. Even as it left his boot he knew it was destined for the top corner and he heard the crowd erupt with excitement.

What you need to know

1. Know how to explain why something is funny.
2. Use terms like exaggeration, sarcasm and word play.

WHAT MAKES THIS FUNNY?

> *still in my room*
> *still raining*
> *still Sunday*
>
> **11.30 a.m.**
> *I don't see why I can't have a lock on my bedroom door. I have no privacy; it's like Noel's House Party in my room. Every time I suggest anything around this place people start shaking their heads and tutting. It's like living in a house full of chickens dressed in frocks and trousers. Or a house full of those nodding dogs, anyway I can't have a lock on my door is the short and short of it.*
> *"Why not?" I asked Mum reasonably (catching her in one of the rare minutes when she's not at Italian evening class or at another party).*
> *"Because you might have an accident and we couldn't get in," she said.*
> *"An accident like what?" I persisted.*
> *"Well you might faint," she said.*
> *Then Dad joined in, "You might set fire to your bed and be overcome with fumes."*
> *What is the matter with people? I know why they don't want me to have a lock on my door, it's because it would be a first sign of my path to adulthood and they can't bear the idea of that because it would mean they might have to get on with their own lives and leave me alone.*

(*Angus, Thongs and Full-Frontal Snogging: Confessions of Georgia Nicolson* by Louise Rennison)

- Georgia writes as if she is very knowledgeable about life, but you soon pick up the clues that she is a teenager.
- The reader is able to learn personal things without it seeming odd, because she is writing in her diary.
- The language adds humour: it is 'still' raining; the adults are described as 'chickens dressed in frocks and trousers' or 'nodding dogs'.

EXPLAINING HUMOUR

- When you explain how something is funny, you need to look for:
  - funny characters and situations;
  - unexpected consequences;
  - exaggerations/sarcasm;
  - double meanings/puns/**word play**.

READING: APPRECIATING HUMOUR

1 Look at this extract from another Georgia Nicolson story. Focus on the humour. On a separate sheet, comment on how the writer's use of language engages the interest of the reader. What does the language tell us about the character? Comment on descriptions, images, style and how she addresses the reader.

Sunday July 16th my room

6:00 p.m.

Staring out of my bedroom window at other people having a nice life. Who would have thought things could be so unbelievably pooey? I'm only fourteen and my life is over because of the selfishosity of so-called grown-ups. I said to Mum, "You are ruining my life. Just because yours is practically over there is no reason to take it out on me."

But as usual when I say something sensible and meaningful she just tutted and adjusted her bra like a Russian roulette player. (Or do I mean disco thrower? I don't know and, what's more, I don't care.)

If I counted up the number of times I've been tutted at, I could open a tutting shop. It's just not fair.... How can my parents take me away from my mates and make me go to New Zealand? Who goes to New Zealand?

In the end, when I pointed out how utterly useless as a mum she was, she lost her rag and SHOUTED at me.

"Go to your room right now!"

I said, "All right, I'll go to my ROOM!! I WILL go to my room!! And do you know what I'll be doing in my room? No you don't, so I'll tell you! I'll be just BEING in my room. That's all. Because there is nothing else to do!!!!!"

Then I just left her there. To think about what she has done. Unfortunately it means that I am in my bed and it is only six o'clock.

(On the Bright Side, I'm Now the Girlfriend of a Sex God: Further, Further Confessions of Georgia Nicolson by Louise Rennison)

SHAKESPEARE: UNDERSTANDING LANGUAGE

What you need to know

1. Know the features of Shakespeare's language.
2. Know how it is the same as language today.
3. Know how to read the plays.

SHAKESPEARE'S PLAYS

- As Shakespeare's plays were written for performance, the best thing to do is to go and *see* a version of the play – either at the theatre or one of the film versions.
- Remember that Shakespeare's work has survived 400 years of performance. This is because most of his plays have **simple, timeless themes** such as ambition, revenge and love.
- His work is *not inaccessible*; you just need to approach the language with an open mind and have fun with your reading.

THE LANGUAGE

- Shakespeare wrote in **blank verse** and **prose**. Verse means poetry (blank means with no rhyme scheme) and prose means 'normal' writing, i.e. in paragraphs.
- Blank verse gives the language its rhythm.
- Prose is used for comic effect or to show the difference in social status between characters (lower class characters speak in prose).
- Two forms of the word 'you' are used. Thou is the familiar form and you is the formal or polite form.
- Shakespeare uses a lot of **imagery**, with characters talking in metaphor and using personification. This is a rich language, descriptive and visual and means that Shakespeare is able to compress a lot of detail into a short space.

MACBETH
Macbeth, Act 4 Scene 1

Thy crown does sear mine eye-balls.

- He uses a lot of **word puns** and **plays on words**, i.e. playing with meaning and deriving comedy from this.

> **BEATRICE**   Foul words is but foul wind, and foul wind is but foul breath,
> and foul breath is noisome; therefore I will depart unkissed.
> (*Much Ado About Nothing*, Act 5 Scene 2)

1 Read the following extract from *Much Ado About Nothing* (Act 2 Scene 3) and answer the questions below. Remember that Benedick thinks that he is hiding here. He does not realise that this is all a trap.

LEONATO	No, nor I neither; but most wonderful that she should so dote on Signor Benedick, whom she hath in all outward behaviours seemed ever to abhor.
BENEDICK	Is't possible? Sits the wind in that corner?
LEONATO	By my troth, my lord, I cannot tell what to think of it; but that she loves him with an enraged affection – it is past the infinite of thought.
DON PEDRO	May be she doth but counterfeit.
CLAUDIO	Faith, like enough.
LEONATO	Oh God, counterfeit! There was never counterfeit of passion, came so near the life of passion as she discovers it.
DON PEDRO	Why, what effects of passion shows she?
CLAUDIO	Bait the hook well; this fish will bite.
LEONATO	What effects, my lord? She will sit you – you heard my daughter tell you how.
CLAUDIO	She did, indeed.
DON PEDRO	How, how, I pray you? You amaze me; I would have thought her spirit had been invincible against all assaults of affection.

(a) Why is it so strange that Beatrice should 'dote on Signor Benedick'?

_____

_____

(b) "Sits the wind in that corner?" is a metaphor. What does Benedick mean by it?

_____

_____

(c) Don Pedro questions whether Beatrice may be 'counterfeit'. What does this mean?

_____

_____

(d) Comment on Claudio's line "Bait the hook well, this fish will bite."

_____

_____

_____

_____

(e) Don Pedro's line, "How, how… against all assaults of affection," gives us insight into how Beatrice's character is perceived. What comment are they making about her here? Why do you think they are doing so?

_____

_____

_____

_____

What you need to know

1   Identify key words and ideas.

SUMMARISING A TEXT

- You need to be able to identify the most important points of a text. You might want to **summarise** them to ensure that you have understood it. Writing down the key points will also help you to write a response to the text.

- The following points summarise the article below. Each one 'sums up' the key point of each paragraph.

> 4000 letters - Greenpeace's message - Public support for wind farms - Climate change (severe weather conditions) - Alternative to nuclear power as a solution

25 August 2004

Letters from 4 000 people supporting a local wind farm were presented to West Somerset District Council this afternoon.

Greenpeace collected the letters at street stalls and festivals, to be given to Council Chief Executive Tim Howes. The message – act now to fight global warming or prepare for the worst.

Some local opposition groups have demanded that planning for the turbines be refused, but the thousands of letters asking the council to give the plan the go-ahead, point out that extreme weather linked to climate change killed 35 000 people in Europe last year and that wind farms are a vital part of the solution to the global warming crisis. Electricity from the Hinkley turbines could power as many as 20 000 homes.

A period of public consultation ends on Friday, when the fate of the proposed wind farm will be passed to the Council Planning Committee, due to report at the end of the year. Views expressed by the public are likely to play a key part in the final decision.

Local Greenpeace campaigner Steve Krupa said: "We've been collecting these letters across the region and beyond for several weeks. You only need to look at what happened in Cornwall this month to realise how important it is to fight climate change. Most people know that if we don't exploit wind energy, we'll end up with a new generation of nuclear power stations, with all the waste, threat to human health and expense that nuclear power has always entailed. The level of support out there for the Hinkley wind farm as part of the solution to climate change is massive."

Greenpeace, 2004 © Greenpeace www.greenpeace.org.uk

1 Look again at the article on page 35. Suggest a headline for it. Then write a brief summary of what it is about in less than 100 words.

_____

_____

_____

_____

_____

_____

_____

_____

_____

_____

2 Read the article below. Firstly, underline the energy sources that are listed. Then write down one sentence that you feel sums up the content of the article. Finally, suggest a title for the article.

Over the course of the last century the world has become increasingly dependent on oil for its power supplies, but there is now a growing realisation that these reserves are going to run out soon and we need to find new sources of energy.

We also need to learn from the lessons of the past. We have burned forests and coal and exhausted the planet's supplies and now we are doing the same with oil. The next generation has to seek out renewable forms of energy that are not dependent upon a quantifiable reserve.

That is why wind energy, solar power and tidal power are coming into their own. These resources require a high initial investment but can then deliver over a long period without running out or damaging the environment. They are the future.

_____

_____

_____

_____

WRITING: TO INSTRUCT

What you need to know

1 Appreciate how to keep instructions clear and easy to follow.

2 Understand the importance of sequencing instructions.

3 Know how to form the imperative.

INSTRUCTIONS MUST BE CLEAR

- Instructional texts are easy-to-follow, step-by-step guides to carrying out a task. If **instructions** are well written, the reader will be able to complete the task perfectly, without becoming confused. Therefore *every* instruction – however obvious – needs to be listed.

- Instructions use the **imperative** form of the verb. That means a command. You form the imperative by using the present tense, without the subject.

> Go... / Take... / Bring... / Adjust... / Wind up... / Attach...

- The instructions below describe how to check and adjust your bicycle. The imperative instructions are in bold. Watch out for terminology, that is the specialist words that you need to know. A diagram or a glossary would help with these.

To adjust the handlebars

1 **Place** the bicycle in an upright position, with one leg either side of the front wheel, and **hold** the front wheel firmly in position.

2 **Loosen** the handlebars using the spanner supplied and **adjust** the handlebars to the right height and position to use. The mid-section of the handlebars must be aligned with the front wheel.

3 **Tighten** into place.

To adjust the position of the saddle

1 The ideal saddle position should allow the toes to touch the ground comfortably. **Loosen** the nut on the main units situated at the bottom of the seat post and **adjust**.

2 Once you have adjusted the seat to the position of your choice, **tighten** into place.

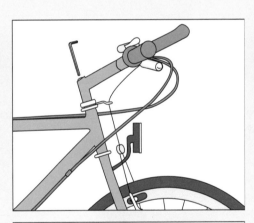

- Instructions may be numbered if this will add clarity.

WRITING: TO INSTRUCT

1 Write a set of instructions for someone who does not know how to reach your home from school.

_____
_____
_____
_____
_____
_____
_____
_____

2 Recipes are instructions. Write a recipe for making cheese on toast, macaroni cheese or another meal of your choice.

_____
_____
_____
_____
_____
_____
_____
_____
_____

3 Write a set of instructions for someone who has never played your favourite computer game.

_____
_____
_____
_____
_____
_____
_____
_____

What you need to know

1. Understand the use of the question mark and exclamation mark.
2. Understand the use of the colon and semi-colon.

USING CORRECT PUNCTUATION

- Effective and accurate punctuation helps any reader to understand what you write. If you do not use it correctly, your writing will not make sense.
- Remember that every sentence *must* start with a **capital letter** and end with a **full stop**, unless it ends with a question mark, an exclamation mark or a colon.

QUESTION MARKS

- A **question mark** is used at the end of any sentence that is a question.

  Why are you hiding in here?
  What is the capital city of France?
  Who is the Prime Minister?

EXCLAMATION MARKS

- An **exclamation mark** shows that the voice of the speaker is likely to be shouting or excited.

  Walk, don't run!
  Look out!
  Don't step off the pavement!

COLONS AND SEMI-COLONS

- The **colon** and **semi-colon** are less common, but you will need to know how to use them.
- The colon has three uses:
  - to introduce a list;
  - in place of a full stop if two sentences are very closely related. The second half usually explains or adds to the first half of the sentence;
  - before a quotation or an example as it is here:

  Bond ran over to the car: a 1980 Aston Martin with bullet-proof shields.

- The semi-colon is useful for complicated lists. You would start the list with a colon and separate the items with a semi-colon:

  At the reception, we had a lovely meal: spinach soup or salmon for starters; turkey, roast potatoes, vegetables and all the trimmings; jelly and ice cream for dessert.

1 Write out the following sentences, adding punctuation marks. You may also need to consult your earlier work on speech marks (page 23) and commas (page 29).

(a)   will wind power deliver our energy needs in the future what do you think

_____

_____

(b)   danger of death keep away

_____

_____

(c)   as the sails of the windmill turn they drive a shaft a heavy wooden cylinder which uses gears to turn the grinding wheel

_____

_____

_____

(d)   emergency shouted the lookout what is it cried the Captain an iceberg sir a huge iceberg he replied

_____

_____

_____

2 Punctuate the following text. The line breaks and capital letters have been left in for you.

It has been an interesting year what with the school blowing away in the tornado and all said Mrs Crumbs as she picked fussily through the selection of biscuits on the china plate in front of her turning her nose up at every single one and finally settling on a custard cream
Well I think it is amazing how you all coped the reporter gushed looking up from her notepad peering out from behind her glasses and nodding her head enthusiastically as she spoke
Yes this is an amazing group of young people we have here Mrs er what was your name again
Wainright Leah Wainright
That's right Weah Lameright How could I forget
The children standing around their headmistress all tried to stifle a grin at the mistake she had made That was one of the things they loved about Mrs Crumbs she always managed to get her words wrong
Was it always an accident they wondered Looking at the mouse-like vision of Leah they were not so sure Yet somehow the old girl always managed to pull it off without causing any *real* offence

WRITING: TO PERSUADE

What you need to know

1 Recognise the features of persuasive writing.

2 Know how to use them in your own writing.

THE PURPOSE OF PERSUASIVE WRITING

- The purpose of a persuasive text is to try to bring the reader round to your way of thinking or point of view.

  Examples of persuasive texts:

  - advertisements;
  - promotional or publicity texts;
  - charity appeals;

  - party political pamphlets;
  - letters to a newspaper;
  - 'comment' column in the newspaper.

- Look at this example of a letter written by a boy who is trying to persuade his parents to let him change schools.

Dear Mum and Dad

Is it not true to say that the happier a student is in their learning environment the more likely he is to succeed? ← **Use of rhetorical question**

Well, if you want me to do well at school, you will have to let me go somewhere else to study. There are several very straightforward reasons for this. ← **Present tense**

Use the first person ('I') →
Firstly, the textbooks here are old, tatty and out-of-date. I am sure you will agree that this is not the best way to ensure my good grades!

Makes use of lists →
Secondly, we never seem to have the same teacher in maths from one lesson to the next. This is disruptive and confusing as I am unable to follow the work.

Uses short, dramatic sentences for impact →
Thirdly, I am not happy. I am being bullied and my computer has been broken by some older boys. This is, as I'm sure you can imagine, highly distressing. ← **Uses emotive language**

I promise that if you let me come home I will work extra hard and always do my best. ← **Addresses the reader directly**

I love you very much and look forward both to your response and a happier learning environment. ← **Employs repetition**

Your beloved son,
James

WRITING: TO PERSUADE

1 Look at this example of persuasive writing. Read through it, underlining the places where the language is persuasive.

Dear Sir/Madam

I am writing to say how sorry I am that the council has decided to support the wind turbine scheme. If this proposal goes ahead we will have to put up with this unsightly tower for years to come. Do you not agree that our children deserve a future that is not blighted by such a monstrosity?

There are three good reasons for rejecting the plan. Firstly, it will be noisy, day and night. The pensioners who live nearby will find it hard to sleep. Secondly, not everyone in the village wants the wind turbine, so building it will divide the village and split our friendly community in half. And, finally, it will not benefit everyone. Only the people in the new estate will be helped and that is simply not fair.

I urge everyone to ask the council to think again. If we all complain, then they are bound to listen!

Yours faithfully

2 School trips in the summer term have been banned for your school year because they are thought to be unsafe and are not sufficiently educational. On behalf of your class, write a letter to the head teacher asking her to change her mind and let your class go to Alton Towers. Continue on a separate sheet.

WRITING: USING QUOTATIONS

What you need to know

1. Recognise when to quote from a text.
2. Understand how to quote correctly.
3. Appreciate different ways of using quotation in your writing.

WHEN TO QUOTE

- Whenever you are writing about another text (that you have not written), you need to provide **evidence** (**quotes**) to support the points that you make. You *show* your reader what you mean by referring to the text in this way.

HOW TO QUOTE

- You can use quotes in two ways.

  - Include the text in your own writing like this:

    The first time we meet the 'fearful man' Magwitch, the description offered by Dickens is very visual. The 'great iron on his leg' adds to this threatening image…

  - Mark off your own writing with a colon, leave a line before the **quotation** and then indent it. Do not use this as an excuse to write really long quotes – choose the relevant part of the text. Don't overdo it!

    In 'Macbeth' the 'weird sisters' are made to seem frightening. Their language is full of spells. We see this in Act 1 Scene 3 as they chant:

    > *'Thrice to thine and thrice to mine*
    > *And thrice again, to make up nine.'*

EXPLAIN THE QUOTE

- Without an explanation your quote is not worth very much. You need to take the point you make further by commenting on the quote you choose.
- Remember the rule: **P**oint, **E**vidence, **E**xplanation (**P, E, E**).

The first time we meet the 'fearful man' Magwitch, the description offered by Dickens is very visual. The 'great iron on his leg' adds to this threatening image.

This means that the reader is able to feel afraid of Magwitch, which creates tension and allows us to empathise with poor Pip.

Point
Evidence
Explanation

WRITING: USING QUOTATIONS

1 Look back to the Ann Bancroft text about Antarctica on page 25. Fill in the missing text in the paragraphs below. You will either be giving the **point**, the **evidence** or the **explanation**.

(a) The writer uses strong images in her writing. She describes the evening hour as a 'flirtation' between the sun and the horizon, saying that they are 'like lovers who gaze at each other across a room but never touch'. This image works particularly

well because _____

_____

_____

(b) Bancroft uses _____

_____

_____

We see this as she describes 'violet' cloud, the 'streaks of sapphire blue', the 'white-capped mountains', the mountain's 'black, rounded humps' and even the 'bit of red in the rocks'. This creates a visual feast for the reader. The colours enable us to visualise the scene – it is vivid and strong.

(c) The writer invites us, the reader, to see through her eyes, as she switches into the second person (you) at the end of the extract.

_____

_____

_____

This makes the relationship between the reader and the writer stronger, as it is almost as if she is speaking directly to us. We are very much 'put into her place' and can almost see through her eyes.

2 Take any article from a newspaper or magazine and write some complete comments, with evidence and explanation, as above. Use the following as a framework for the points you make.

  A Look at the relevance of the heading/title.

  B Are you able to tell the writer's point of view or not? Is it biased?

  C What effects are created by the language?

  D One more point that you feel is relevant to your chosen article.

_____

_____

_____

_____

WRITING: ON THE COMPUTER

What you need to know

1. Understand the terms: regular, italics, bold, underlining, font size.
2. Appreciate how to use a computer to edit your work.

FONTS

- You should choose a **font** that is easy and clear to read and one that suits the purpose of your writing. Avoid very large or very small fonts.
- You can use **bold**, *italics* and <u>underlining</u> when you want to *emphasise* key words or *stress a particular point*.

SPACING

- Think about how you want to present your work. You may wish to 'centre' a poem on the page. For an essay or story, 'justifying' your writing is better.
- Always leave a line between paragraphs to make sure that your writing does not look cramped on the page.

EDITING

- One advantage of working on a computer is that you are free to **edit** (change/redraft) your work at any stage.
- If you have written a story and you re-read it, you may decide that something is missing. If it could do with some more description, move the cursor to the place where you want to insert the text – even a whole new paragraph – and type it in. It's easy!
- You can also swap around the order of your paragraphs by using the 'cut' and 'paste' functions. Highlight the text, then cut it and paste it into its new location. It's much easier than writing the whole thing out again!

Cut   Paste

- Remember, if you make a change (for example, deleting something you didn't want to) you can use the 'undo' function.

Undo

- Make sure that you **save** your work from time to time, otherwise you might lose it all!

Save (Ctrl+S)

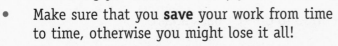

Times New Roman ▾	**B**	*I*
Font	Bold	Italic

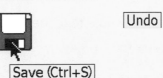

Justify   Centre

WRITING: ON THE COMPUTER

1 Look at this unedited piece of writing. Mark the changes you would make to it on a computer. Mark in the paragraph breaks. Underline with a wiggly line the key words you would put into a bold font. Underline with a straight line any words you would put in italics.

Facts about wind turbines

An upwind turbine like the General Electric 3.6 Megawatt Prototype is designed to operate facing into the wind but they can be designed to run downwind, facing away from the wind as well. Most turbines have either two or three blades. Wind blowing over the blades causes the blades to lift and rotate. A controller starts up the machine at wind speeds of about 8 to 16 miles per hour (mph) and shuts off the machine at about 65 mph. Turbines cannot operate at wind speeds above this because their generators could overheat. There is a disc brake, which can be applied mechanically, electrically, or hydraulically to stop the rotor in emergencies. More usually, the blades are turned, or pitched, out of the wind to keep the rotor from turning in winds that are too high or too low to produce electricity. The towers are made from tubular steel. Because wind speed increases with height, taller towers enable turbines to capture more energy and generate more electricity.

2 You need to use a computer for this activity.

Type out the article above and make the changes you have marked.

Try the cut and paste functions, experimenting with moving the paragraphs around to change the order.

Highlight and delete the whole text, then select undo to bring it back again.

What you need to know

1 Understand the purpose of a story opening.

2 Recognise opening features and techniques for engaging the reader.

THE PURPOSE OF A STORY OPENING

- In a **story opening**, the writer will **engage the reader** by describing one of the following:
  - a character – the reader gets to know the protagonist straight away;
  - the setting (the place) – the reader can picture the scene and feel 'there';
  - an event – the reader is instantly thrown into the action.
- The opening will include powerful language – images and description – as well as clues as to what might happen.

- This opening is from *Holes*, by Louis Sachar.

There is no lake at Camp Green Lake. There once was a very large lake here, the largest in Texas. That was over a hundred years ago. Now it is just a dry, flat wasteland.

There used to be a town of Green Lake as well. The town shrivelled and dried up along with the lake, and the people who lived there.

During the summer the daytime temperature hovers around ninety-five degrees in the shade. There's not much shade in a big dry lake.

The only trees are two old oaks on the eastern edge of the 'lake'. A hammock is stretched between the two trees, and a log cabin stands behind that.

The campers are forbidden to lie in the hammock. It belongs to the Warden. The Warden owns the shade.

Out on the lake, rattlesnakes and scorpions find shade under the rocks and in the holes dug by the campers. Here's a good rule to remember about rattlesnakes and scorpions: If you don't bother them, they won't bother you.

Usually.

Sometimes a camper will try to be bitten by a scorpion, or even a small rattlesnake. Then he will get to spend a day or two recovering in his tent, instead of having to dig a hole out on the lake.

But you don't want to be bitten by a yellow-spotted lizard. That's the worst thing that can happen to you. You will die a slow and painful death.

Always.

READING: STORY OPENINGS

1 Answer the following questions on the extract from *Holes* on page 47.

(a) What can you comment about the first line of the book,
'*There is no lake at Camp Green Lake.*'?

_____

_____

_____

_____

(b) Would you say that the setting is a welcoming or a hostile one? How do the animals mentioned affect it? What mood/atmosphere is created? Use examples from the text to support your answers.

_____

_____

_____

_____

_____

(c) What is the effect of the words '**Usually**' and '**Always**'?

_____

_____

_____

(d) What impression do we get of the Warden in this extract? Give evidence to support your answer.

_____

_____

_____

2 Now write the opening extract to a story set at your school. Someone is going to be murdered later in the story and you need to set the scene and create the right atmosphere, without giving away anything that is going to happen. Continue on a sheet of paper.

_____

_____

_____

_____

PUNCTUATION: APOSTROPHES AND PLURALS

What you need to know

1. Understand the correct use of the apostrophe.
2. Know how to use nouns in the plural form.

CORRECT PUNCTUATION AND GRAMMAR

- Correct punctuation and grammar are essential. This section provides you with a quick check on some of the areas where students often make mistakes.

APOSTROPHES

- **Apostrophes** are used either to show ownership or to indicate where two words have been joined and a letter is missing (a contraction). They are *never* used to show that a noun is in its plural form.

  I borrowed Daniel's computer to write my essay.

  Ownership: computer belonging to Daniel

  That's a good idea. He won't mind anyway, he's your brother.

  Contractions: That is/will not/he is

- This table should help. Notice that the apostrophe *always* goes where the letter is missing.

will not	won't
shall not	shan't
cannot	can't
is not	isn't
do not	don't
ought not	oughtn't
must not	mustn't
I will	I'll

PLURAL NOUNS

- Normally, to make a noun **plural** (more than one), you add '**s**'.

  phone → phones   bed → beds

- When a noun ends in '**s**' or '**ch**', you add '**es**' to make it plural.

  church → churches   kiss → kisses

- When a noun ends in a '**y**', you make it plural by changing the '**y**' into an '**i**' and adding '**es**'.

  lady → ladies   pony → ponies

- There are irregular nouns as well, which follow no standard pattern.

  sheep → sheep   man → men

PUNCTUATION: APOSTROPHES AND PLURALS

1 Write the following phrases in their contracted form (using an apostrophe).

(a)   You will never be able to eat all of those.

_____

(b)   Will it not be too expensive if we all go?

_____

(c)   It does not matter what time it is.

_____

(d)   I cannot be bothered to go all the way up there.

_____

(e)   I ought not to have another biscuit.

_____

(f)   I must not be late.

_____

2 Fill in the plural forms of the nouns in the table below.

Singular	Plural
horse	
butterfly	
witch	
sheep	
foot	
clock	
woman	
bus	

What you need to know

1. Understand the features and principles of newspaper articles.
2. Recognise the importance and the effect of word choice.

FEATURES OF NEWSPAPER ARTICLES

- **Newspaper articles** should be unbiased.
- They have a very factual style.
- They are written with the minimum wording, so that the reader can understand the gist of the article by reading only a short piece.
- The opening paragraph is called the 'nose' and needs to contain all five 'W' questions: Who? What? Where? Why? When?
- This is a newspaper front-page story about a demonstration against the proposal to ban hunting with dogs.

What? ———→ THE great countryside uprising to defend foxhunting ran out of control and provoked a security nightmare as protesters stormed the chamber of the House of Commons and police fought with others outside.

Who?

Where?

When? Armed police were last night guarding the chamber after the extraordinary invasion during the debate on the Hunting Bill by five demonstrators wearing white pro-hunt T-shirts who evaded all Parliament's security checks to reach the floor of the House.

Why? Their action provoked outrage among MPs, who would have been defenceless had the men had any violent intent. It succeeded in bringing proceedings to a halt for 20 minutes. The incursion came about an hour before MPs voted overwhelmingly — and almost certainly for the last time — to ban foxhunting.

EFFECT OF STRONG LANGUAGE

- Look at the words highlighted in bold in the newspaper article. This language is about combat and war; it gives the article impact, without actually saying 'it was like a war in the Commons last night'.

WRITING: LANGUAGE CHOICE

1 Write your own 'nose'. Test how good your writing skills are by dramatising a really commonplace event that is not harmful at all. Use 'the language of war' (examples are given below) to give your article impact and make the event sound really dramatic. Answer all five 'W' questions. Write about the following event:

Getting up to walk across the room to turn over the TV channel, because the remote control was not working.

fought	struggled	battled	contest	resistance	surrender	defeat
wounded	injured	brave	skirmish	dogfight	attack	defence

_____

_____

_____

_____

_____

_____

_____

_____

_____

_____

_____

_____

_____

_____

_____

_____

_____

WRITING: TO DISCUSS

What you need to know

1. Understand the purpose of discursive writing.
2. Recognise the features of discursive writing.

THE PURPOSE

- Discursive writing is used in formal essays or in any analysis or evaluation of an idea, product, solution or performance.

- In discursive writing, you are discussing a point, so your writing needs to be **balanced**. Your writing should literally weigh up both sides of the argument, giving equal consideration to each. Your argument should flow logically from one 'side' to the other.

THE STRUCTURE

- Start with a statement of the issue to be discussed. This can often be taken from the title. Then say what you are going to discuss and why. This acts as a preview to your main arguments.

- The main body takes the form of a for-and-against argument. Supporting evidence must be offered for both sides of the argument – and the writer should not be seen to favour one view personally.

- Finish with a recommendation, given in the form of a summary of the main points, and then a conclusion.

THE FEATURES

- Discursive writing:
  - should be in the present tense;
  - should not include the personal pronoun 'I' (except in the conclusion). Use clauses like 'It could be argued that...' or 'It is clear that...' instead;
  - should include logical connectives, such as: therefore, thus, because, and as a result;
  - should use connectives which indicate a change of direction or comparison: on the other hand, however, in addition, alternatively, conversely.

> **Remember**
> Connectives are very important when linking ideas between paragraphs.

WRITING: TO DISCUSS

1 You have been asked to write a piece which outlines the arguments for and against the council's plan to build a wind turbine to supply energy to a housing estate. You need also to draw conclusions.

Here is the complete list of arguments:

- It will be noisy.
- It will only benefit the people on the estate.
- There is one in a nearby village already.
- Wind power is clean and leaves no waste.
- It will look ugly.
- The turbine will put the village on the map.
- It will be visible for miles.
- It is the power of the future.
- If it failed or went wrong there could be a disaster.
- It will take a year to build.
- It will attract tourists and benefit the local post office.
- It was planned two years ago so people have had plenty of warning.
- The local council opposes the scheme.
- Just over half of the villagers have signed a petition opposing the scheme.

Write the report providing a balanced discussion of this issue. Continue on an extra piece of paper if you need to.

WRITING: BUILDING ON DESCRIPTIONS

What you need to know

1. Understand the importance of elaborating on descriptions.

2. Recognise the need to use strong words in your writing.

3. Be prepared to describe minute detail.

BUILDING THE LAYERS

- You need to be able to play with language and have fun with it. You also need to be able to *show* your reader what you are describing. You have seen this on pages 7 and 25.

- Building more layers into your description will make your writing even more readable and engaging.

- If you want the reader to feel that she/he is 'there', in the text, you need to ensure that the reader can feel and visualise what you are describing. You can do this in the following ways:

  - expand your description by giving examples – **elaborate**;

  - use **strong verbs** where possible so that sentences have impact;

  - use **strong adjectives** to describe the nouns you use;

  - recount **minute details**, to focus the reader's eye on a specific thing or to affect him/her in a specific way;

  - create **visual images** so that the reader can get a strong visual sense of the scene you are describing.

- Below is another extract from Ann Bancroft's Antarctica expedition (strong verbs are in bold):

I was as close as I'd ever been to **breaking**, emotionally and physically. My knees ached so badly that I wanted to **groan** out loud with each step. The pain had become a constant presence, often causing tears that froze inside my goggles. The temperature **hovered** at -15°F (-26.1°C), but the harsh wind made it feel much colder. Exposed human flesh here would freeze in less than a minute. I **longed** for the relative warmth of the Minnesota winter I was missing back home. The Antarctic cold **tortured** the new pink skin on my cheeks, **peeled** raw by the intense sun and bitter wind. But at least I could still feel my feet. And how? With each downhill step, my toes **jammed** into the ends of my boots. I knew from experience that when I pulled off my socks that night, my toes would be purpled knobs. I would lose all my blackened toenails in a few days. Still, that was better than frostbite.

| Example/elaboration |
| Personification |
| Elaboration/minute detail |
| Elaboration |
| Visual images |
| Details |

(*No Horizon Is So Far* by Ann Bancroft, Liv Arnesen and Cheryl Dahle)

55

WRITING: BUILDING ON DESCRIPTIONS

1 Choose a stronger verb as an alternative for each of the following:

moved along _____   called out _____   looked _____

2 Read Liv's account of her broken sled and then answer the questions.

> I was sick of my sled. The tow bar, a short ladder section made from titanium meant to keep the sled in line at a set distance behind me, had broken shortly after we began our trek, so I was pulling my sled with a rope. There was nothing to stop the sled from drifting from side-to-side or crashing into me. When I headed downhill, my sled came chasing after me and slammed into my legs if I did not leap out of the way fast enough. I started to think of the sled as a living thing, an animal stalking me, waiting for my weak moments. Sometimes, I could feel it shimmying behind me, jerking against the rope like a wild horse. I became very good at hearing the sound of the runners skittering on the ice as the sled attacked. I could tell whether it was coming from my left or right, and then jump! – just as it was about to hit me.

(a)   What was wrong with the sled?

_____

(b)   Liv compares the sled to a dangerous animal. Show how Liv's language expresses this. Quote from the text to support your answer.

_____

_____

_____

_____

_____

_____

3 Write a description of an object you own that annoys you because it does not work properly. In your description, give the object animal qualities to bring it to life and describe its movements/appearance/function. Write on a separate piece of paper. Use the space below to make notes and brainstorm your answer.

_____

_____

_____

_____

_____

_____

What you need to know

1 Know how to answer questions involving careful reading.

2 Understand how to use information in answers.

3 Recognise the difference between fact and opinion.

READING FOR DETAIL

- It is one thing to understand what a piece of writing is generally about, but it can be more difficult to answer questions on detail.

- When you are reading for detail, you need to look closely at the text. It is not enough to understand the gist. You may need to read an article several times and look very closely when answering any questions.

- The article below shows you that detail can be complicated – you need to pay attention!

American Thomas Stoddard holds the world record for the longest ever career with the same firm. He started in the post room at the Speakman Company pipe-fitting firm in Delaware on February 16, 1928 when he was 16. He worked his way up until he retired from the board of directors 75 years later on February 16, 2003, aged 91.

(*Metro*, 20 October 2004)

What was Stoddard's position at the firm when he retired?

- Stoddard worked in the post room.   ✗

Stoddard started in the post room but was on the board of directors when he retired.

- Notice all the facts and figures in the article below! If you were going to answer questions on this, you would need to read the text very carefully for each answer to make sure that you were answering correctly.

Crime trauma for half of teenagers

Half of 11 to 16-year-olds have been victims of crime or aggression and one in five knows someone who carries a knife, a survey revealed yesterday. One in three has been bullied, nearly one in four has been abused by a stranger in the street and one in four has been a victim of a mobile phone theft, according to the study of 550 youngsters by insurer Norwich Union and charity Crime Concern. More than half wanted tougher jail terms for the culprits.

(*Metro*, 20 October 2004)

1 Read the following article and then answer the questions below.

Natural disasters 'on the rise'

More and more people are being caught up in a growing number of natural disasters, a United Nations agency said on Friday.

Events including earthquakes and volcanoes, floods and droughts, storms, fires and landslides killed about 83 000 people in 2003, up from about 53 000 deaths 13 years earlier. There were 337 natural disasters reported in 2003, up from 261 in 1990.

The problems are made worse because more and more people are living in concentrated urban areas and in slums with poor building standards and a lack of facilities. Urban migrants tended to settle on exposed stretches of land either on seismic faults, flooding plains or on landslide-prone slopes.

"The urban concentration, the effects of climate change and the environmental degradation are greatly increasing vulnerability," one expert said. "Something has to be done now".

ISDR

(a) Find **three** types of natural disaster associated with unusual weather.

_____

_____

(b) Since what year has there been a 30 000 increase in deaths resulting from natural disasters?

_____

(c) Look at these four statements. According to the article, **two** are true and **two** are false. Put a tick next to those that are true.

A	Everyone is equally at risk from natural disasters.	
B	More people are living in areas prone to flooding.	
C	Climate change is a cause of natural disasters.	
D	Earthquakes are the biggest killers of all natural disasters.	

(d) In paragraph 2, who is the writer describing with the term 'urban migrants'?

_____

(e) From the whole article, find **one** fact and explain **one** personal opinion.

Fact	Personal Opinion

(f) What is the meaning of 'urban concentration'?

_____

_____

WRITING: SPELLING STRATEGIES

What you need to know

1 Recognise some of the spelling pitfalls.

2 Use tricks to make spelling more accurate.

TIPS FOR GOOD SPELLING

- It is useful to expand your vocabulary and sometimes you may want to use a word that you have heard but not seen written down. It is good to try to use longer words but sometimes you may have to take the risk of misspelling them. The best thing you can do, is to look new words up in a **dictionary** to make sure that your spelling is correct.

- It is very important that you get **key words** right. Spelling key words incorrectly looks clumsy and the mistakes tend to be repeated when you use the word several times.

- You may find that you have a 'mental block' with some words, and that you never know how to spell them. Make a list of these words and keep them with you as you revise.

- **Chunking** is a good way to help you to spell a tricky word. To do it, break a word down into the little words that make it up.

  in – finite – ly   cool – ly   develop – ment

- Use little rhymes and sayings called **mnemonics** to help you remember.

  Necessary and successful: It's necessary to have only one 'c' but to be successful you need two!

- Thinking of **words that rhyme** with the tricky one can sometimes help too.

  thread – dead, instead, read, bread

- Some people think about **words as families** and remember that they have family resemblances.

great	great-er	great-ness	great-est	
quiet	dis-quiet	un-quiet	quiet-er	quiet-ness

Remember

Don't forget to use a **dictionary**. Looking up words regularly and then writing them down several times really will help you to remember them next time you want to use them.

WRITING: SPELLING STRATEGIES

1 Look closely at these pairs of words and decide which is the right spelling for each one. If you're not sure, use a dictionary to help you. Write down the correct answer and then learn the list.

1   irresistible **OR** irresistable   _____

2   alright **OR** all right   _____

3   separate **OR** seperate   _____

4   harrass **OR** harass   _____

5   pursue **OR** persue   _____

6   reccomend **OR** recommend   _____

7   seize **OR** sieze   _____

8   cemetary **OR** cemetery   _____

9   definately **OR** definitely   _____

10   ocasion **OR** occasion   _____

11   drunkenness **OR** drunkeness   _____

12   occurence **OR** occurrence   _____

13   weird **OR** wierd   _____

14   alot **OR** a lot   _____

15   poem **OR** peom   _____

16   embarrassment **OR** embarassment   _____

17   repetition **OR** repitition   _____

18   accidently **OR** accidentally   _____

19   existence **OR** existance   _____

20   privilege **OR** priviledge   _____

21   imature **OR** immature   _____

22   relative **OR** relitive   _____

23   illegal **OR** ilegal   _____

24   incredible **OR** incredable   _____

25   accomodation **OR** accommodation   _____

26   flexible **OR** flexable   _____

27   critisise **OR** criticise   _____

28   tommorrow **OR** tomorrow   _____

29   happyness **OR** happiness   _____

30   atall **OR** at all   _____

READING: UNDERSTANDING STRUCTURE

What you need to know

1 Know how writers plan and organise their writing.

2 Know how they write for specific purposes and audiences.

STRUCTURE EXAMPLE

- This is the start of an account by Virginia Reed Murphy of her family's journey across America to a new life in California. As you read it, notice the way that the writer has organised the text so that you are drawn into her story.

> this sets the context and 'dangers and ordeals' interests the reader

Although I was only twelve years old when my family began its journey to California, I remember the trip well. I have every reason to do so, since the dangers and ordeals we faced were so extraordinary.

> 'ill-fated' suggests an exciting story and the date gives the account a time

Our little band, which drove out of Springfield, Illinois, on April 14, 1846, has often been referred to as the "ill-fated Donner party." All the previous winter, we prepared for the coming journey.

> this is a shift in the narrative but the reader is being prepared for something to come

One of my main concerns was encountering Indians, the very thought of which frightened me no end. Grandma Keyes had an aunt who had been taken prisoner by the Indians in an early settlement in Virginia and had remained a captive in their hands for five years. Evening after evening, I would go into Grandma's room and sit with my back close against the wall so that no warrior could slip behind me with a tomahawk. I would coax Grandma to tell me more about her aunt, and I would listen to the recital of the fearful deeds of the Indians until it seemed to me that everything in the room, from the high old-fashioned bedposts down to the shovel and tongs in the chimney corner, had been transformed into Indians in paint and feathers, all ready for the war dance.

Our wagons were all made to order, and I can say without fear of contradiction that nothing like our family wagon ever started across the plains. It was a two-story wagon that some called a "pioneer palace car." We also had two wagons loaded with provisions. My father started with supplies enough to last us through the first winter in California, if we made the journey in the usual time of six months. Knowing that books were always scarce in a new country,

> back to the narrative, building up the excitement around the journey

we also took a good library of standard works.

We had many animals with us: five dogs, saddle horses, cows, and oxen. The family wagon was drawn by four yoke of oxen and the other animals were led or herded along as we made our way to California. I also had a pony. His name was Billy, and he was a beauty. The chief pleasure I looked forward to when crossing the plains was to ride my pony every day. But a day came when I had no pony to ride. The poor little fellow gave out, for he could not endure the

> from describing the animals we now find ourselves on the trail sharing Virginia's feelings over the loss of her horse

hardships of ceaseless travel. When I was forced to part with him, I cried until I was ill, and I sat in the back of the wagon watching him become smaller and smaller as we drove on, until I could see him no more.

(Across the Plains In The Donner Party - 1846–47 by Virginia Reed Murphy)

READING: UNDERSTANDING STRUCTURE

1 Answer the following questions in response to the text on page 61.

(a) Can you give **two** reasons why paragraph 1 makes a good introduction to this text?

_____

_____

_____

(b) In paragraph 2, what do the words 'ill-fated' suggest?

_____

(c) How do you think Virginia felt about embarking on the journey to California? Quote from the text to support your answer.

_____

_____

_____

_____

(d) Find **three** words or phrases that give a frightening impression of the Indians. Quote each one and say why it creates a frightening picture.

_____

_____

_____

_____

_____

(e) Tick these sentences if they are true.

A	Virginia's pony died on the journey.	
B	Grandma Keyes had been captured by Indians.	
C	The family travelled light with only the essentials.	
D	The trip usually took six months.	

(f) What makes the final paragraph particularly effective?

_____

_____

_____

_____

PUNCTUATION: VERBS, OBJECTS AND TENSES

What you need to know

1. Recognise parts of a sentence.
2. Know how to form the past and future tenses.
3. Recognise irregular forms of the past tense.

PARTS OF A SENTENCE

- A sentence can be broken down into its parts. In order for a sentence to be complete, it must contain a **verb** (which must have a **subject**) and a **direct object**.

Jamie	kicks	the ball
↑	↑	↑
subject	verb	direct object

  - The verb is the action/doing word.
  - The subject is the person or thing 'doing' the verb.
  - The (direct) object is what the verb refers to.

- A sentence may also have an **indirect object**. An indirect object is another element that relates to the verb, with a preposition.

Jamie kicks the ball to Luke   ←   indirect object

- You can tell the indirect object because it is, or could be, preceded by a preposition, such as: by; with; to; through; from.

FINITE VERBS

- The **finite verb** in a sentence is the verb that tells you what tense the action is/was/will be happening in.

Jamie **will be** playing with his football later.
↑
finite verb

- **'Playing'** is the action in this sentence, but it is not the finite verb. It does not tell us **when** Jamie plays. The finite verb is the verb **'to be'**, here in the future tense.

Jamie **will play** with his football later.

- Here, the finite verb is **'to play'** in the future tense, because it tells us **when**.

TENSES

- To form the future tense, you simply add 'will' before the verb:

will go   will see   will have   will tidy

- To form the past tense, you add (in most cases) the past participle 'ed' to the end of the verb:

played   passed   climbed   sorted   looked

- However, some verbs are irregular, so watch out!

to be – was   to have – had   to know – knew   to fly – flew   to blow – blew

63

PUNCTUATION: VERBS, OBJECTS AND TENSES

1 Circle the part of each sentence which is given in brackets.

(a)   (finite verb) Shameen always knew what she wanted to do.

(b)   (direct object) Stuart liked to play the drums.

(c)   (subject) Janie was a very good student.

(d)   (indirect object) Daniel took his sick dog to the vet.

2 Read the following sentences and decide whether they are happening in the past, present or future. Write out the sentences, putting the verb in the correct tense each time.

(a)   It (to be) a really hot day tomorrow, according to the weather report.

_____

_____

(b)   I always (to think) that skateboarding looked easy, until I had a go!

_____

_____

(c)   I (to like) eating ice cream and I always will.

_____

(d)   What do you want to do when you (to grow up)?

_____

(e)   What do you think David Beckham wanted to be when he (to grow up)?

_____

_____

(f)   My brother (to eat) too many sweets, so he was sick.

_____

3 Complete the table of irregular verbs with the past tense.

to grow	
to hold	
to run	
to see	
to bring	
to think	
to sing	
to hang	
to take	
to read	
to make	

WRITING: TO EXPLAIN

What you need to know

1 Recognise the features of explanatory texts.

2 Appreciate how explanation differs from information.

FEATURES OF EXPLANATORY WRITING

- Sometimes, **explanation** and **information** are very similar. Information texts tell the reader the facts. Explanation texts go a little further.

- Explanation texts answer the questions 'How?' or 'Why?' and attempt to teach the reader something new. The writer teaches what he or she knows as a series of linked stages. Much of the writing you encounter in science lessons is explanatory, working from what you know to knowledge that is new.

These could all be explanatory writing:

  - an account of how the gears on a bike work;

  - a letter explaining how a game at school got out of hand;

  - a report on a plane crash showing why the accident happened.

- Explanation texts use time connectives such as **then**, **next** and **after** or **causal connectives** such as **because**, **however**, **as a result**, **therefore**.

- In this explanation of what causes wind, notice how words like **because** help to make the writing clearer.

Wind is caused by air flowing from areas of high pressure (where cooler air is descending) to areas of low pressure (where warmer air is rising). Because the Earth is rotating, however, the air does not flow directly from high to low pressure, but it is deflected to the right (in the Northern Hemisphere; to the left in the Southern Hemisphere), so that the wind flows around the high and low-pressure areas.

The closer the high and low-pressure areas are together, the stronger the winds. Near the surface of the Earth, friction from the ground slows the wind down.

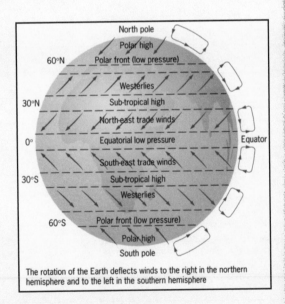

The rotation of the Earth deflects winds to the right in the northern hemisphere and to the left in the southern hemisphere

Because high and low areas are cooler or warmer than their surroundings, wind is also the way that the atmosphere moves excess heat around. All wind is, directly or indirectly, helping to transport heat either away from the surface of the Earth, where sunlight causes an excess of energy, or from warm regions (usually the tropics near the Equator) to cooler regions (usually the higher latitudes). Where the earth is hottest in the tropics more extreme winds such as monsoons and hurricanes form because of the heat.

WRITING: TO EXPLAIN

1 Write an explanation of what causes earthquakes. This summary will help you, but you must link the facts using your own connectives so that it flows as an explanation text.

Earth has hard crust / molten rock underneath / crust made up of plates that slowly push against each other / mountain ranges form where plates meet pushing up land / faults are the unstable edges of the plates / pressure of molten rock moves the plates / can build up close to where mountains form / these are earthquake areas / molten rock sometimes forced to the surface / as volcano / molten rock at the surface of the Earth is called lava

_____

_____

_____

_____

_____

_____

_____

_____

_____

_____

_____

_____

_____

_____

_____

_____

_____

_____

_____

_____

_____

_____

_____

_____

What you need to know

1 Be able to find the right answer by careful reading.

2 Avoid distracting items.

THE VARIOUS QUESTION TYPES

- Multiple-choice questions give you a choice of answers (A, B, C or D), where only one of the answers will be correct (unless the question states otherwise).

- Some questions give you a choice of statements that are **true** or **false**, and ask you to decide which are which.

- Some questions might ask you to fill in a series of boxes or to fill in missing information to complete a table or diagram.

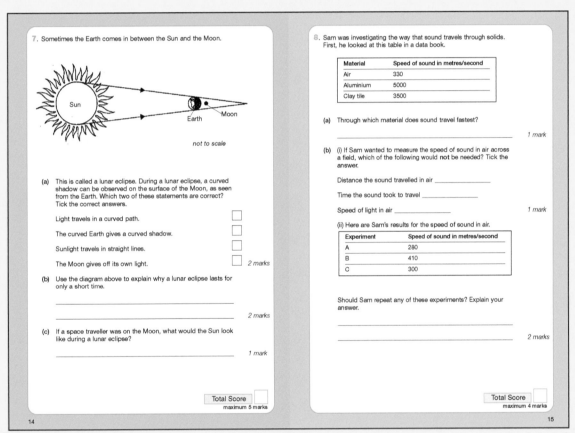

(from Collins Revision Guides: *Practice Papers KS3 Science*)

READING QUESTIONS CAREFULLY

- Watch out for statements that are partly right or seem, at first reading, to be right – they are put there to distract you! Make sure that you do not just read a statement through quickly and then jump to your answer. Re-read the statement several times and make sure that you are satisfied with your response.

- Do not rush your reading of the text. That is the first thing that will risk you getting answers wrong. Make sure that you feel comfortable and familiar with the text *before* you begin to answer questions on it. That way you are less likely to be caught out by questions that seem obvious but are there to trick you.

1 Read the following passage and then answer the questions.

Hurricanes are intense low-pressure areas that form over warm ocean waters in the summer and early autumn. Their source of energy is water vapour which is evaporated from the ocean surface and then condenses to form clouds and rain, warming the surrounding air. When there is little wind this heat can build up, causing low pressure to form. The low pressure and the rotation of the Earth near the tropics causes wind to begin to spiral inward toward the centre of the low. These winds help to evaporate even more water vapour from the ocean, spiralling inward toward the centre, feeding more showers and thunderstorms, and warming the upper atmosphere still more.

Circle the correct response to each question.

(a)   According to the extract, which of these is true?

A Hurricanes are associated with warm ocean waters and spring.

B Hurricanes are associated with warm ocean waters and summer.

C Hurricanes are associated with cool ocean waters and spring.

D Hurricanes are associated with cool ocean waters and autumn.

(b)   Which of these words could replace 'intense' in line 1?

A hot

B powerful

C stormy

D immense

(c)   A hurricane could not develop without:

A water

B wind

C heat

D low pressure

(d)   Which of these titles could best describe the content of this article?

A The killer storms

B Midsummer storms

C High pressure hurricanes

D How a hurricane grows

WRITING: CHANGING TENSES

What you need to know

1 Use the present, past and future tenses.

2 Understand how writers use tense change for effect.

USING TENSES IN YOUR WRITING

- A good general rule about **tenses** is not to change them as you write. Keeping your writing in the same tense is most effective. It is bad style to mix up tenses and can leave your reader very confused, for example:

  It was a very dark night but I can see the stars shining brightly in the sky.

  Can you tell if this is happening in the past or the present? What is this writer doing?

CHANGING TENSES FOR EFFECT

- Sometimes writers change tense for effect. For example, changing from the past tense to the present in story writing can add excitement and another layer of reflection. Look at this example.

  I am ordinarily a very strong person and not a scaredy-cat at all, but I do remember one occasion when I really had cause to be scared. I was about 12 years old and had been visiting my Granny in Cornwall, I knew that something strange was going on, because…

- This writer talks (as narrator) to the reader in the present and then starts to reflect on something that happened in the past. Switching between tenses in this way can be a very good narrative device, creating rich characters and experiences. It can give a text a lot of depth.

- The present tense can add excitement because the reader feels that they are actually there. The present tense is used in 'as-it-happens' news reporting – usually on television. The reporter will often address the viewer directly. For example:

  I am standing here in Trafalgar Square and even the sun decided to come out to welcome home the British Olympic team. As you can see, the atmosphere here is incredible, we've got a whole cross-section of the British public here today, come out to celebrate the outstanding achievements of British Olympians and Paralympians.

- This is a different style from that used in newspapers, which are reporting on an event, after the event. Newspaper articles are, therefore, normally written in the past tense. For example:

  Trafalgar Square was amass with well-wishers and fans yesterday, as Central London was opened up to welcome home the British Olympic team. Even the sunshine came out to show support to the scores of medallists from this year's Olympic Games.

WRITING: CHANGING TENSES

1 A dormant volcano has erupted and you are the first news reporter on the scene. Write your television news story in the present tense.

_____

_____

_____

_____

_____

_____

_____

_____

_____

_____

_____

_____

_____

_____

_____

2 Now write the same story for a newspaper article the following day. Use the past tense and remember to include: Who? What? Where? Why? When?

_____

_____

_____

_____

_____

_____

_____

_____

_____

_____

_____

_____

_____

_____

_____

_____

What you need to know

1 Appreciate how to read a poem to get the most out of it.

2 Understand how to comment on a poem.

DON'T PANIC AT POETRY!

- A poem is a way for a writer to express personal, often complex, ideas to the reader by creating images and provoking an emotional response.

- The best way to read a poem is to read it aloud to yourself. Then, read it through a second time, making notes on a piece of paper of any feelings or images that come to you. Try not to use your brain too much when you read a poem. Just relax and read it and see what thoughts and feelings come.

- Read a poem over and over again. Each time new ideas will come to you.

- In the poem below, the phrases in **bold type** are there to help you make sense of it. They also help you see what the poet is trying to say. Look back at page 21 for tips on **poetry terms** to help you do the activities on page 72.

> **All those times I was bored**
> out of my mind. Holding the log
> while he sawed it. Holding
> the string while he measured, boards,
> distances between things, or pounded
> stakes into the ground for rows and rows
> of lettuces and beets, which I then (bored)
> weeded. Or sat in the back
> of the car, or sat still in boats,
> sat, sat, while at the prow, stern, wheel
> he drove, steered, paddled. **It
> wasn't even boredom, it was looking,**
> looking hard and up close at the small details. Myopia. The worn gunwales,
> the intricate twill of the seat
> cover. The acid crumbs of loam, the granular
> pink rock, its igneous veins, the sea-fans
> of dry moss, the blackish and then **the graying
> bristles on the back of his neck.**
> Sometimes he would whistle, sometimes
> I would. The boring rhythm of doing
> things over and over, carrying
> the wood, drying
> the dishes. Such minutiae. It's what
> the animals spend most of their time at,
> ferrying the sand, grain by grain, from their tunnels,
> shuffling the leaves in their burrows. **He pointed
> such things out**, and I would look
> at the whorled texture of his square finger, earth under
> the nail. Why do I remember it as sunnier
> all the time then, although it more often
> rained, and more birdsong?
> I could hardly wait to get
> the hell out of there to
> anywhere else. Perhaps though
> boredom is happier. It is for dogs or
> groundhogs. **Now I wouldn't be bored.**
> Now I would know too much.
> **Now I would know.**   *Margaret Atwood*

READING: APPRECIATING POEMS

1 Write down some of the images and ideas that came to you as you read Atwood's poem on page 71.

_____

_____

_____

_____

_____

2 What would you say is the mood of this poem? Explain your answer and support it with **one** quote from the poem.

_____

_____

_____

_____

_____

3 What are **three** of the 'boring' things the writer used to find herself doing?

_____

_____

_____

_____

_____

4 What do you think she means when she says the following lines?

'It wasn't even boredom, it was looking,
looking hard and up close at the small
details.'

_____

_____

_____

5 Quote **three** details about her father.

_____

_____

_____

6 What do you think Atwood 'would know', looking back on her childhood?

_____

_____

_____

WRITING: HOMOPHONES

What you need to know

1 Understand that words can sound alike but have different meanings.

2 Recognise that homophones are spelled differently.

WHAT ARE HOMOPHONES?

- **Homophones** are words with different meanings and different spellings but they are spoken identically. This is not a problem in speech, or when you read, because the context makes what you mean obvious.

  Today, we are at the air base watching the new stealth fighter emerging from its reinforced concrete hangar.

The coat fell on the floor as he took it off the hanger.

- However, when you are writing, you have to remember which word to use. Are you looking at a geyser shooting hot water into the air on your holidays or is that geezer looking at you? When you are looking at the window, are you thinking about your idol or just being idle?

- The words below are all pronounced in exactly the same way.

  pause   paws   pores   pours

- Notice how they do not have the same meaning. They are homophones (homo = same, phone = sound).

  Let's take a pause.   The cat has four paws.   To prevent spots, clean your pores.
  In this country, when it rains, it pours!

WRITING: HOMOPHONES

1. Each of these words has a homophone. Complete the table with words that sound the same, but are spelled differently.

Word	Homophone	Word	Homophone
assent		bale	
lightning		horse	
medal		great	
night		navel	
overseas		paced	

2. Now use each of the words in the completed table in a short sentence to show what it means.

_____

_____

_____

_____

_____

_____

_____

_____

_____

_____

_____

_____

_____

_____

_____

_____

_____

_____

_____

What you need to know

1 Be able to tell fact from opinion.

2 Know how to identify opinion.

THE DIFFERENCE BETWEEN FACT AND OPINION

- The difference is that **facts** can be verified – checked up on to see if they are correct – but **opinions** never can. Opinions tell you about someone's belief, an idea they have, or a feeling.

- The following examples are taken from a football match report.

Opinions

- The game was the most exciting of the day.
- The second goal was scored from a superb diving header.
- Everyone says that Liverpool deserve to be champions.

Some people would rather have been watching their own teams than Liverpool; others might think that the diving header was a lucky bounce after the player fell over, and no-one but Liverpool fans want their team to win anything! These are all opinions.

Facts

- Keino, the Nigerian centre-forward, scored the first goal.
- Liverpool won 2-0.

The name of the goal scorer and the final score can easily be verified. Therefore, they are facts.

THE LANGUAGE OF OPINION

- You can pick out an opinion from a fact by looking at the language that expresses it. Look out for:
  - words that carry judgements: exciting, favourite, best;
  - words that qualify: probably, certainly, always, never;
  - words that link to beliefs: think, believe, claim.

READING: FACTS AND OPINIONS

1 Read this article and then decide whether the statements that follow are fact or opinion. Ring the correct answer for each one.

> £250 000 has already been spent on rebuilding the school after last year's disastrous fire, but some people believe that the modern computer facilities with a screen for every child and the state-of-the-art classrooms will quickly be wrecked by the pupils. The headteacher knows that this will not happen if the teachers are quick to impose firm discipline, but the dinner ladies are not so sure!

(a) Last year's fire was a disaster for the school.   **FACT / OPINION**

(b) Firm discipline will stop the school from being damaged. **FACT / OPINION**

(c) There is a computer screen for each child.   **FACT / OPINION**

(d) The dinner ladies do not know anything.   **FACT / OPINION**

(e) The cost of rebuilding is at least £250 000.   **FACT / OPINION**

2 Now write **three** of your own facts and **three** of your own opinions.

Facts:

1 _____

_____

2 _____

_____

3 _____

_____

Opinions:

1 _____

_____

2 _____

_____

3 _____

_____

READING: ADVERTISEMENTS

What you need to know

1 Recognise what an advertisement is selling.

2 Understand how advertisements work.

WHAT IS AN ADVERTISEMENT?

- An **advertisement** is like a persuasive text. It has been created in order to sell you a **brand** (product). You see advertising everywhere: on television, in magazines, on billboards, in direct mail and through sponsorship (football, for example).

- Where you see an advert is never an accident; the location, time, style and approach of the advertisement have all been specifically chosen in order to access the **target audience** (the people to whom they are trying to sell the product).

HOW DOES ADVERTISING WORK?

- An advertisement will try to sell you a product by convincing you that something is 'true'. It could be that buying this product will make you feel better, lose weight, be happier or have a nicer home. The 'true' thing is sometimes called the **promise**.

- Advertisers also work with the concept of 'creating need'. This means that once you believe that the product is all that it claims it is, you will then feel that you need it.

- Adverts combine **copy** (words), **graphics** (pictures) and various sales/marketing techniques to make you agree. The techniques that will make you believe the promise and buy the product include:

  - **getting aboard** – everyone has one and if you don't get on the bandwagon, you'll be left out;

  - **transferring** – using the product will make you more like the happy, attractive and appealing person in the advert;

  - **associating** – this product is linked to fun enjoyable times, places and activities.

- To make these techniques work, adverts use **emotional language** to provoke feelings in you. These can be negative (for example, being left out, lonely, frightened) or positive (for example, feelings of power, excitement, success, being part of a lively group).

- A lot of advertising is **concept advertising**. It uses **imagery** – the pictures and illustrations – to appeal to you. These images can be disconnected so that they may not have much to do with the product (for example: toothpaste – icebergs; orange drink – fun with your mates) but when you see the advert you link them in your mind. When concept advertising is used, particularly on television, sometimes you do not even know what the advert is selling until the very end of the advert, but you already have been swept along by the **image** of the **brand**.

READING: ADVERTISEMENTS

1 Think about a television advertisement you have seen recently and analyse it by completing the table below.

Brand	
Music	
Time and channel	
Characters	
Images/events/story it shows	
Language	
Target audience	
Overall effect created	

2 Design your own advertisement for a teenage magazine. The advert is to sell a new hair product that is a conditioning gel for both boys and girls and which has tiny glittery stars in it.

Give the product a name. Think hard about the associations you want to make and the image you want to create. Annotate your advert to show the effects you want to create.

Use the space below to make notes, but use a separate piece of paper for your advert.

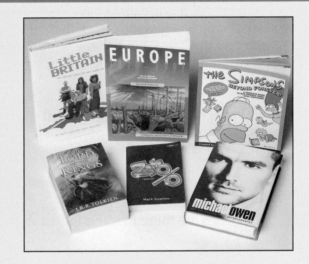
What you need to know

1. Know how reading is linked to genre.
2. Know how to recognise common genres.

DIFFERENT STYLES OF WRITING

- In a typical school day you could find yourself reading all sorts of different materials – a storybook or a play in English, an informative book about earthquakes in Geography and a book explaining how we lived in the past in History.

- Texts vary according to type or purpose and they also divide into different styles or **genres**.

Fiction

thriller	adventure	romance	comedy	historical fiction
fantasy	science-fiction	mystery/detective	horror	

Non-fiction

biography/auto-biography	encyclopaedia	travel	reference books
guides/advice	news stories/eye witness accounts		

- Each genre has its own specific style and features. For example, a comedy novel will use very different language and images to a horror novel.

GENRE-PLAY

Distillation is the preferred procedure for prising apart two liquids in a mixture. You force the innocent liquid into a closed container – where there is no way out, nowhere for the mixture to escape – and then turn up the heat. The mixture will begin to struggle and bubble, but you must show no mercy, waiting and watching until one of the liquids boils and is forced to transform into vapour. Collect this vapour, allowing none of it to escape, and cool it. The vapour will now condense – it cannot help itself – and it is then a pure liquid, and all yours! You can use this same torture – I mean, method – to rip a liquid away from a contented mixture of liquid and solid.

- See how the language a writer uses can change the effect of a text! The text above is an adapted explanation from a science textbook. The genre is now horror or thriller writing, and rather different from the original style!

- The text could be written as an adventure text, or even a romance. The effect that you want the language to have on the reader is dependent on the genre that you write in.

1 Read the following non-fiction text, the introduction to the autobiography of a successful performer.

Turning 60, as I did last week, and qualifying for my free bus pass, I can say that I feel I have reached an age where I am ready to share some of the experiences of this life that I have been blessed with. Not just the career, the glitter and the lights, but the low points, the tears and the anguish. Life is not easy, no matter who you are.

I was born during the Blitz, at the end of World War 2, whilst Londoners were being bombed relentlessly and the skies were lit up every night with searchlights and the glow of burning buildings. The falling bombs shook the foundations as my mother, brother Tony and sister Susan camped out on the platform of the Tube along with hundreds of other families from the East End (many our neighbours and friends). It was on a night such as this, on the platform at Bethnal Green, that I came singing and dancing out of my mother and into the world…

(a) What clues are there that this is an autobiographical text?

_____

_____

(b) Explain how the text would be different if it were a biography. Write the first line.

_____

_____

_____

_____

(c) What title would you give to the book, given the facts in the extract above?

_____

2 Re-write this science text in a genre of your choice. See page 79 for a list of genres. Think about the adjectives you use and choose powerful verbs that suit your genre.

If a person tries to walk on deep snow, they will sink further into the snow than someone wearing skis. When a person wears skis, their weight is spread over a larger area than for someone wearing shoes. Therefore the pressure is low and they can move easily over the top of the snow.

_____

_____

_____

_____

_____

WRITING: REVIEWS

What you need to know

1 Understand what makes a good review.

2 Know how to structure a review.

THE PURPOSE OF A REVIEW

- A book, film or CD **review** has two purposes:
  - to describe something so that people can see if they are interested in it;
  - to evaluate it, i.e. to say how good it is and whether you would recommend it.

WHAT MAKES A GOOD REVIEW?

- In a review, you should set out to interest and inform your readers and then give them a considered personal opinion. You have to be careful to **evaluate** and not to summarise the contents or retell the story. One way to do this is to think of your book review as answering a number of questions. These include:
  - What was the purpose in writing this book and who is it for? Is it interesting for these people?
  - How appropriate is the book's title? Does it promise what the book delivers?
  - What is the genre of the book and what are its main themes?
  - What are the book's most striking textual features?
  - Is the book well written, easy to read and easy to follow?
  - What qualifications does the author have for writing on this subject?
  - How does the book compare with others known to you on the same subject or by the same author?
  - What is your personal response? Is it satisfying to read? Is it convincing? Why? If not, why not?
- Make notes as you read and as you write your review, use them to back up the points you are making. Organise your points in a logical order and remember that the evaluation you make should be supported by evidence – examples from the book or quotations.
- When you write your final draft of a review, remember to include full details of the book's title, the author and the publisher, to help your readers to buy a copy.
- Remember not to give too much of the story away though. Read the short text below as an example of how you can avoid falling into the 're-telling the story' trap.

Cider with Rosie is a fascinating account of childhood in a rural setting, seen through the eyes of our narrator and protagonist, Laurie. The heart-warming account of Lee's childhood and awakening into adulthood takes the reader through a range of experiences and encounters with different characters, not least with Rosie, who gives her name to the title of this charming pastoral novel. Lee's style lends itself to...

WRITING: REVIEWS

1 Write a review of a book you have recently read.

OR

2 Write a review for a teenage magazine of a film that you have seen. Use the guidelines on the previous page, but remember that you will be talking about a piece of cinema, not a book, so you will need to mention the script, direction, cinematography and performances of the actors.

Make notes to help you before you start and use the questions on page 81 to prompt your writing.

WRITING: COMMON MISTAKES

What you need to know

1 Appreciate common mistakes in English.

2 Understand how to avoid making them.

HOW TO AVOID COMMON MISTAKES

- In your writing, try to avoid making the following very common mistakes. (Look back through this book to refresh your memory, if you need to.)
  - Always use a full stop at the end of a sentence, unless it is a question (use a question mark) or an exclamation (use an exclamation mark);
  - Break up parts of a sentence using commas;
  - Open a list with a colon;
  - Begin a new paragraph after a change of time, place, action, idea or speaker;
  - Read the question properly – do not rush your reading or your answers;
  - Do not use repetitive language – vary your use of verbs and adjectives;
  - The correct form of the conditional past tense is 'could *have* done...' NOT 'could *of* done...';
  - An apostrophe marks ownership or a missing letter due to contracting two words. It is NEVER used for plural forms of nouns;
  - Quote evidence from a text to support your points and use quote/speech marks to do so;
  - Check your writing for spelling mistakes.

Open a list with a colon...separate items in the list with semi-colon... .

HANDWRITING

- Your handwriting can let you down, too – if it is not tidy it may be illegible.
- Check that the tops and tails of letters are clearly defined and that your writing is neither too slanted nor cramped. Also, if you have got into the habit of writing little circles for full stops or adding smiley faces, now is the time to stop!

1 Write these short paragraphs **three** times, once using your normal handwriting style and then twice more, trying out improvements and variations.

When you sit with a nice girl for two hours, you think it's only a minute. But when you sit on a hot stove for a minute, you think it's two hours. That's relativity.
Albert Einstein

_____

_____

_____

_____

_____

_____

Parents can only give good advice or put them on the right paths, but the final forming of a person's character lies in their own hands.
Anne Frank

_____

_____

_____

_____

_____

_____

2 Now it is time to be your own worst critic. Look back over all the work that you have done in this book. Take a different coloured pen and mark any mistakes that you see. Use the checklist on page 83 to help you.

Be hard on yourself – it is the only way that you will learn! Reviewing and evaluating your own work is an excellent way to spot your weak areas. This will enable you to improve them.

Read the following texts and then answer the questions which follow.

TEXT A

Wind power – at what cost?

It is a cold wet autumn morning in a peaceful village in East Anglia but it is anything but quiet. Around a hundred residents are barracking a group of developers, council officials and local councillors. There are placards, leaflets and a lot of arguing and shouting. But these are not your typical agitators. They are wealthy looking men and women, sleek and comfortable in their waxed jackets and expensive coats done up against the rain. They have nice haircuts and golfing umbrellas, and it is their big cars – not those of the council group – which are parked along the road. There is not a nose ring nor a wedge of braided hair in sight. These are the English middle classes on the move and what they are complaining about is a proposal to park three massive wind turbines on the edge of their village.

For Ben Ackroyd and Susie Bedford this is NIMBYISM in action. As environmental campaigners they are normally used to standing on the other side of the police line but today they are trying to sell the idea that wind power is good to a group of disgruntled villagers.

"If it was nuclear power, then I'd understand," says Ben, "but this is something safe and effective."

"The problem is," adds Susie, "that these people are the big consumers of power – just look at those cars – and they don't mind paying for it but they don't think about the effects of their actions."

Ben and Susie are soon at work, trying to get into the thick of the debate and to make the villagers see that there is more to this debate. It is clearly hard work!

"What they can't see," says Ben, "is that if they don't have a wind farm – and everyone else feels the same about their local area – we shall be back to the nuclear option or increasing our dependence on oil."

After a couple of hours, the group from the council leaves, promising to take the views of the villagers into account. The demonstrators look content as they get into their cars. They have made their point and unlike a lot of demonstrators, they have the money and influence to back it up. Susie confides that she thinks that they are going to win. The scheme will be rejected by the council and then it is back to the drawing board. This little village has saved its view of the horizon but at what cost to the environment, the climate and the future of the planet?

Hydrogen – a new source of power?

Fossil fuels such as gasoline, diesel and coal all produce airborne pollutants. Some of the major pollutants created from these fossil fuels are carbon dioxide, carbon monoxide, nitrogen oxide and methane. All of these pollutants play a major part as culprits behind acid rain and global warming.

Hydrogen fuel is a cleaner alternative to fossil fuels. Wind, solar and hydro power can produce hydrogen fuel that is 100% pollution-free and 100% renewable. Hydrogen can be made from water, and when burned, turns back into water.

How does hydrogen provide energy?

Most of us already know that water is composed of two parts hydrogen, and one part oxygen. To burn the hydrogen to provide energy, the hydrogen atoms are separated from the oxygen atoms through a process called 'electrolysis' and then compressed into fuel tanks. When the hydrogen atoms are subsequently burned as fuel, they recombine with oxygen atoms in the air and turn back into water. Because they do this so effectively the only 'exhaust' from a hydrogen-powered bus would be warm moist air.

Why change to hydrogen fuels?

Huge oil spills are becoming very common, killing all sorts of aquatic life. If hydrogen fuel were spilled in large quantities it would evaporate instantaneously and the only by-product of hydrogen fuel is water.

- Pollution from ships, planes, automobiles and factories has created smog all across the U.S. Hydrogen fuel emits no pollutants that contribute to smog.

- Changing to a hydrogen-based economy would create thousands of new industrial and scientific jobs. Building plants, manufacturing parts and selling equipment would all be investments that stimulate jobs and growth.

- Fossil fuels will eventually run dry. Hydrogen is renewable, therefore it's unlimited.

- Hydrogen fuel is clean and does not contribute to acid rain, ozone depletion or global warming.

Environmental Media North West [http://4hydrogen.com/contact.html]

Recycle now!

Everyone seems to be talking about recycling these days. Recycling and responsible waste disposal have become key issues in recent years, given growing concern over climate change.

Think about the amount of 'rubbish' that you throw away. These days even vegetables come in neat little plastic dishes, wrapped in more plastic. Whether it is tomatoes on the vine, new potatoes, individually wrapped broccoli, plastic bags of carrots or plastic boxes of fruit, everything in our lives seems to come shrink-wrapped with layer upon layer of valuable material. Not to mention bottles, cans, jars, newspapers, magazines and the endless reams of leaflets and junk-mail that litter our doorsteps.

Traditionally, waste is either buried in landfill sites or burned in large incinerators. Plastic is an environmentalist's nightmare. It is non bio-degradable, so it never breaks down and remains as litter forever. Plastic also produces noxious fumes when burned.

Recycling is the obvious solution to this problem and local authorities now provide opportunities for residents and businesses to recycle effectively. The strong message is the three Rs: reduce, reuse and recycle.

How much of the waste you create is avoidable? Do you really need to buy pre-packaged vegetables, for example? Could you avoid or boycott companies and fast-food outlets who use expensive and environmentally damaging packaging?

Instead of buying cans and bottles of fizzy drink, reuse your drinks bottles or take a flask to school. Make your own lunch instead of buying pre-packed sandwiches and reuse carrier bags. Make sure that you do not waste paper – write on both sides and keep paper for scrap. Just think about what you are using and whether you need to throw it away – or whether you could use it again.

Finally, recycle now! Glass, plastic, paper, aluminium, steel and cloth can all be recycled, and uncooked kitchen waste makes excellent compost for the garden or allotment. With a bit of effort, a household can reduce the amount of waste it produces by up to 90%. So there are no excuses. You can make a difference – a big one. So, let's make recycling a national habit and protect our environment for the generations to come.

1. From paragraph 1, give **two** reasons why this demonstration is unusual.

   (i) _____

   (ii) _____

   `2 marks`

2. In paragraph 1, what does the choice of words in the following phrases suggest to you?

   (a) *not a nose ring nor a wedge of braided hair in sight*

   _____

   _____

   `1 mark`

   (b) *sleek and comfortable*

   _____

   _____

   `1 mark`

3. Summarise the argument that Ben and Susie are trying to make to the demonstrators.

   _____

   _____

   _____

   `2 marks`

4. NIMBY stands for Not In My Back Yard. What has this got to do with the demonstration?

   _____

   _____

   `1 mark`

5. Explain why the text uses comments from Ben and Susie in direct speech as well as describing events.

   _____

   _____

   _____

   `2 marks`

6. How would you describe the attitude of the writer of this text to the demonstration, to the environmentalists and to the proposal?

_____

_____

_____

2 marks

Questions 7-II are about the Hydrogen article

---

7. Suggest **two** ways in which the first paragraph uses language to suggest to the reader that fossil fuels are a threat to the planet.
Support each point you make with a quotation.

(i) _____

_____

(ii) _____

_____

2 marks

8. Paragraph 3 provides an explanation of how hydrogen cells work. List **two** features of explanatory writing from the paragraph and give examples to back up what you say.

(i) _____

_____

_____

(ii) _____

_____

_____

3 marks

9. In the section _Why change to hydrogen fuels?_, how are the 'reasons' presented to the reader? What effect does this have?

_____

_____

_____

2 marks

10. In the text as a whole, how is language used to make hydrogen fuel sound like an attractive alternative energy source?

_____

_____

2 marks

11. How does the layout of the article benefit the reader?

_____

_____

2 marks

Questions 12-16 are about Recycle now!

---

12. Paragraph 2 contains a lot of listed information. What effect does it have on the reader? Explain your answer.

_____

_____

2 marks

13. What **two** methods are traditionally used to dispose of waste?

(i) _____

(ii) _____

1 mark

14. Explain the effect of the use of questions in the text.

_____

_____

2 marks

15. Explain the meaning of the following:

(i) noxious _____

(ii) non bio-degradable _____

2 marks

16. Summarise the content of the article in one paragraph.

_____

_____

_____

3 marks

Total 32 marks

PRACTICE WRITING TEST

Section A: Longer Writing Task

You have **45 minutes** in which to plan and write this task. Aim to spend about **15 minutes** on your planning and the rest of the time on your writing. Leave yourself enough time at the end of the task to check your work.

At the doctor's

The waiting room at the doctor's brings together all sorts of people – young and old – from different backgrounds.

Write the introduction to a story which starts where people are waiting to see the doctor and where the lack of spare seats brings together two people from very different worlds.
Describe – the waiting room, its atmosphere, your two characters.
Narrate – what happens, including some lively dialogue.

30 marks

Section B: Shorter Writing Task

You have **30 minutes** to complete this task, including planning time. Try to spend about **10 minutes** on your planning and **20 minutes** on your writing. Leave yourself enough time at the end of the task to check your work.

The advice column of a teenage magazine has received this letter.

There is a girl in my year who I would like to go out with but we have got into this habit of teasing each other and playing jokes so that although we get on in the playground, I don't know if she really likes me or is interested in me. It's been going on like this for a while now and it's left me feeling confused. What can I do?

Ben

Answer the letter by giving your advice. You have to:
- **show understanding and sympathy;**
- **suggest what the writer might do.**

20 marks
(including 4 for spelling)

PRACTICE SHAKESPEARE TEST

Much Ado About Nothing

Act 1 Scene 1, lines 99 to 124

Act 2 Scene 3, line 201 to the end of the scene

Compare the relationship between Beatrice and Benedick in these two extracts. What has changed? Look closely at the language and the way they respond to one another.

Support your ideas by referring to the extracts.

18 marks

Act 1 Scene 1, lines 99 to 124

In this extract, Beatrice and Benedick, who have not seen one another for some time, renew their merry war. Each of them tries to score points off the other during their verbal duel.

BEATRICE   I wonder that you will still be talking, Signor Benedick; nobody marks you.

BENEDICK   What, my dear Lady Disdain! Are you yet living?

BEATRICE   Is it possible disdain should die, while she hath such meet food to feed it as Signor Benedick? Courtesy itself must convert to disdain if you come in her presence.

BENEDICK   Then is courtesy a turn-coat. But it is certain I am loved of all ladies, only you excepted; and I would I could find in my heart that I had not a heart, for, truly, I have none.

BEATRICE   A dear happiness to women! They would else have been troubled with a pernicious suitor. I thank God, and my cold blood, I am of your humour for that: I had rather hear my dog bark at a crow than hear a man swear he loves me.

BENEDICK   God keep your ladyship still in that mind! So some gentleman or other shall scape a predestinate scratch'd face.

BEATRICE   Scratching could not make it worse, an 'twere such a face as yours were.

BENEDICK   Well, you are a rare parrot-teacher.

BEATRICE   A bird of my tongue is better than a beast of yours.

BENEDICK   I would my horse had the speed of your tongue, and so good a continuer. But keep your way a God's name, I have done.

BEATRICE   You always end with a jade's trick; I know you of old.

Act 2 Scene 3, line 201 to the end of the scene

In this extract, Benedick has just overheard Don Pedro, Leonato and
Claudio talking of Beatrice's 'love' for him. Then Beatrice enters and
Benedick reacts to her according to his new 'knowledge'.

BENEDICK [*coming forward*] This can be no trick: the
conference was sadly borne. They have the truth of
this from Hero. They seem to pity the lady: it
seems her affections have their full bent. Love me!
why, it must be requited. I hear how I am censured:
they say I will bear myself proudly, if I perceive
the love come from her; they say too that she will
rather die than give any sign of affection. I did
never think to marry: I must not seem proud: happy
are they that hear their detractions and can put
them to mending. They say the lady is fair; 'tis a
truth, I can bear them witness; and virtuous; 'tis
so, I cannot reprove it; and wise, but for loving
me; by my troth, it is no addition to her wit, nor
no great argument of her folly, for I will be
horribly in love with her. I may chance have some
odd quirks and remnants of wit broken on me,
because I have railed so long against marriage: but
doth not the appetite alter? A man loves the meat
in his youth that he cannot endure in his age.
Shall quips and sentences and these paper bullets of
the brain awe a man from the career of his humour?
No, the world must be peopled. When I said I would
die a bachelor, I did not think I should live till I
were married. Here comes Beatrice. By this day!
she's a fair lady: I do spy some marks of love in
her.

*Enter **BEATRICE***

BEATRICE Against my will I am sent to bid you come in to dinner.
BENEDICK Fair Beatrice, I thank you for your pains.
BEATRICE I took no more pains for those thanks than you take
pains to thank me: if it had been painful, I would
not have come.
BENEDICK You take pleasure then in the message?
BEATRICE Yea, just so much as you may take upon a knife's
point and choke a daw withal. You have no stomach,
signior: fare you well.

Exit

BENEDICK: Ha! 'Against my will I am sent to bid you come in
to dinner' – there's a double meaning in that 'I took
no more pains for those thanks than you took pains
to thank me.' That's as much as to say, Any pains
that I take for you is as easy as thanks. If I do
not take pity of her, I am a villain; if I do not
love her, I am a Jew. I will go get her picture.

Exit

ANSWERS TO ACTIVITIES FOR WEEKS 1-8

Story basics: elements of texts Week 1 Monday
1(a) False (b) The story is set outside a very sinister and creepy house, surrounded by a thick hedge which has a gap just large enough to look through. It is dark (night), lit up by a flickering street-lamp and raining.
(c) The atmosphere is dark and threatening. The house is eerie and strange and the darkness and rain add to this effect. (d) Jamie is narrating the story. We know this because he refers to himself by name (' "Jamie, you big idiot!" I said to myself.') (e) The text is dark and tense. We feel the tension with 'I held my breath and felt my whole body tense up, my jaw locking, heart nearly missing a beat'. The darkness, threatening environment and hostile weather add to the mood as with the 'twisted branches and thorny undergrowth'. *You could also mention the shadows, the 'strange sounds echoing from the broken door', the 'ugly roar' or 'rain lashing about my face'.* (f) *stooped like a giant ape*

Story basic: characters and descriptions Week 1 Tuesday
1(a) *Your table should be completed to build up one particular character from your imagination.* (b) *Your writing should focus on using interesting adjectives to describe the character and ' show' him/her through illustrating his/her behaviour.*

Story basics: using tension Week 1 Wednesday
1 *Your answer should build up tension throughout the piece. You may include the following: show that your peaceful sleep is disturbed by an unfamiliar noise; emphasise that you are alone; use strong adjectives to describe the noise, your feelings and the atmosphere; mention how you are feeling – show the reader this through describing the effects on your body; describe the journey downstairs using language that illustrates how slowly and carefully you are creeping; describe the noise getting louder as you approach the door; manipulate punctuation and vary sentence length to speed up/slow down the text; make sure the reader is hanging off the edge of their seat by the time you open the door; then end with a climax or anti-climax as you wish.*

Punctuation: paragraphs Week 1 Thursday
1 C, A, D, B. C introduces the reader to the topic of paragraphs; A opens the main discussion of paragraphs and gives the example of change of idea; D expands on A and mentions further occasions when a new paragraph is needed; B discusses the conclusion – it provides a definite finish to the text.
2 *You should have used at least 3 paragraphs. Your writing needs to be fairly impersonal as it is for a website.*

Writing: planning Week 1 Friday
1 *As long as your spider diagram makes sense to you it is right!*
2 *You should have grouped* similar ideas *using the same colour.*
3 *Your ideas should look more like paragraphs now (but with topic headings).*
4 *You should have numbered the paragraphs in a sensible order.*

Reading: retrieving key words Week 2 Monday
1(a) By 'so-called monstrosity' the author means that other people have called the turbine a 'monstrosity' (ugly). (b) whirr (c) elegant, curvaceous.
2(a) propel, pump, grin, generate (b) propel, primitive, isolated (c) Ancient Egyptians used wind power seven thousand years ago. (d) 'Dwellings' means houses or living quarters.

Writing: to inform Week 2 Tuesday
1(i) 'Wind is a form of solar energy': in the present tense
(ii) 'Winds are caused by the uneven heating of the atmosphere by the sun': this fact gives specific information (iii) 'Humans use this wind flow, or motion energy…': uses technical terms. *You could also mention the lack of personal pronouns, or use other examples from the text to illustrate the points above.*
2 *Your writing should include 3 paragraphs, an introduction and a conclusion. You should not have used 'I', and have followed the rules of informational writing on page 17.*

Reading: plays Week 2 Wednesday
1(a) *List the characters in the scene.* (b) *Describe where* that scene *is set.* (c) *Describe the action.* (d) *Describe this scene's relevance to the play as a whole. What do we learn here? How does it affect the rest of the play? Does anything change?* (e) *List themes.* (f) *How are the characters interacting?* (g) *Where are the characters on the stage? What are they doing physically?* (h) *What do the characters actually say?*

Reading: poems Week 2 Thursday
1(a) ABBA, ABBA, CDDECE is the rhyme scheme (b) The theme of the poem is death. (c) 'silent land' means death – or the place you go to be at peace, after dying. (d) The voice seems to be addressing a loved one – specifically a husband – as she says 'You tell me of our future that you plann'd'. (e) The poet says 'do not grieve' if you forget me for a while, because it is better to forget and be happy, than to remember and be sad.

Punctuation: direct and reported speech Week 2 Friday
1(a) Harry asked what time it was. (b) Miss Parker said to slow down because she couldn't hear a word I was saying.
2 (a) "I am sick of that dog at number 42!" said the postman. (b) "I am going ice-skating this evening," said Salma to Louise.
3 uttered, murmured, remarked, exclaimed, whispered, grunted, shouted, proclaimed, muttered, grumbled.
4 *You should have used the following: speech marks, a new line for each speaker, a comma at the end of speech to separate it from the rest of the sentence, exclamation and question marks where necessary.*

Writing: looking again at description Week 3 Monday
1 *You could have underlined any adjectives, metaphors and interesting expressions – of which there are examples in every sentence of the text.*
2 *(Suggested possible answers)* (a) *The wisps of smoke danced through the air.* (b) *Ice formed in sheets and created an ice-rink on the pavement.* (c) *Leaves fell like flame-coloured angels floating gently to the floor.* (d) *The rain danced like glass ballerinas on the sodden stone of the path.* (e) *The cold chill felt like an icy whisper from the underworld.* (f) *Teeming torrents of rain left flowing rivers in the narrow, winding streets of the old town.*
3 *You should have included rich, visual images in your response, used strong adjectives and been careful over word choice. Can you picture the scene as you read it? Is it recreated for you?*

Writing: to argue Week 3 Tuesday
1 *Your writing should be emotive and strong, using rhetorical questions, considered reasons, examples, second-guessing. You could include arguments such as: threat to local environment/habitats, pollution, danger for children, noise, lack of open spaces/play areas, falling house prices, negative effects on physical and metal health.*

Punctuation: commas Week 3 Wednesday
1(a) Mr Flash, who was in the queue for the cash machine, was held up at gunpoint. (b) Red, white and blue are the colours of the Dutch flag. (c) After years of preparation and many tears, she was ready for the longest, most challenging race of her career.
2(a) When he came to the low church wall, he got over it, like a man whose legs were numbed and stiff, and then turned round to look for me. When I saw him turning, I set my face towards home, and made the best use of my legs. But presently I looked over my shoulder, and saw him going on again towards the river, still hugging himself in both arms, and picking his way with his sore feet among the great stones dropped into the marshes here and there, for stepping-places when the rain was heavy, or the tide was in.
(b) At the start of the second half, Woodhead Athletic began to dominate the match.
"Get forward more!" shouted the captain, "Draw the defenders to the wings!" Stuart pushed forward and then, suddenly, a dream ball from Cortez, the young, talented Argentinian centre-back, arrived at his feet. One, two, three steps and Stuart hit the ball running. Even as it left his boot, he knew it was destined for the top corner and he heard the crown erupt with excitement.

Reading: appreciating humour Week 3 Thursday
1 *Your answer should include: the diary style of the writing 'Staring out of my bedroom window…' and chatty way of addressing the reader. Teenager – this comes out in stroppiness and comments like 'you are ruining my life…'. Also the made-up words like 'pooey' and 'selfishosity' add humour and depth to the character. She gets confused with the funny image of 'Russian roulette player/ disco thrower' which suggests she is quoting things she doesn't completely understand. Attempts to take on adult language and style – 'I just left her there. To think about what she'd done'. Uses a lot of exclamation marks!!! Immature style - very expressive of her teenage feelings.*

Shakespeare: understanding language Week 3 Friday
1(a) It is strange that Beatrice should 'dote' on Benedick because it has always seemed on the outside that she cannot stand him. (b) By 'sits the wind in that corner?' Benedick means 'is that the truth?' (c) By 'counterfeit' Don Pedro means Beatrice may not be genuine. (d) Claudio uses the metaphor to describe Benedick (the 'fish'). He means that they should feed Benedick convincing lies because he will fall for them. (e) In this line Don Pedro says that he too believed Beatrice to be incapable of loving ('invincible against all assaults of affection'). Perhaps this makes the case more convincing to Benedick who would also be thinking the same thing. It may also make Benedick feel special.

Reading: summaries Week 4 Monday
1 *Possible headline: '4000 support local solution to global warming'. Summary should include: 4000 support Greenpeace letter; been challenged but turbines offered as vital solution; final decision at end of year; we see the evidence of need to seek alternative energy and there is considerable support.*
2 Underline: oil; forests; coal; wind; solar; tidal. The article discusses the world's dependency upon oil, as with coal and forest before, and urges us to look to renewable sources of energy for the future. Suggested title: *'Lessons of the past must power the future'.*

Writing: to instruct Week 4 Tuesday
1 – 3 *Make sure that your instructions can be followed to the letter.*

Punctuation: question marks and more Week 4 Wednesday
1(a) Will wind power deliver our energy needs in the future? What do you think? (b) Danger of death. Keep away! (c) As the sails of the windmill turn, they drive a shaft (a heavy wooden cylinder) which uses gears to turn the grinding wheel. (d) "Emergency!" shouted the lookout.
"What is it?" cried the Captain.
"An iceberg, sir! A huge iceberg!" he replied.
2 "It has been an interesting year, what with the school blowing away in the tornado and all," said Mrs Crumbs as she picked fussily through the selection of biscuits on the china plate in front of her, turning her nose up at every single one and finally settling on a custard cream.
"Well, I think it is amazing how you all coped," the reporter gushed, looking up from her notepad, peering out from behind her glasses and nodding her head enthusiastically as she spoke.
"Yes, this is an amazing group of young people we have here, Mrs, er, what was your name again?"
"Wainwright. Leah Wainwright."
"That's right, Weah Lameright! How could I forget?"
The children standing around their headmistress all tried to stifle a grin at the

mistake she had made. That was one of the things they loved about Mrs Crumbs – she always managed to get her words wrong!

Was it always an accident? they wondered. Looking at the mouse-like vision of Leah, they were not so sure. Yet somehow the old girl always managed to pull it off without causing any *real* offence.

Writing: to persuade   Week 4 Thursday

1 underline: 'put up with'; 'this unsightly tower'; 'Do you not agree … monstrosity?'; *all of the second paragraph*; 'I urge everyone'; 'If we all … listen!'
2 *Your answer should follow the features of persuasive writing, which are listed on page 41. Also, make sure that your work is paragraphed effectively.*

Writing: using quotations   Week 4 Friday

1(a) …by comparing the scene to love we are able to appreciate its beauty and the magic, the relationship between the sun and the horizon is clear and beautiful, although they are not doing anything. **(b)** …colours to add depth and a visual quality to her descriptions. **(c)** 'For in Antarctica, there is nothing between you and the sky… You can see for hundreds of kilometres…'
2 *Make sure that your writing is structured as instructed.*

Writing: on the computer   Week 5 Monday

1 Paragraph breaks would come at every subject change: 'Most turbines…', 'A controller…', There is a disc brake…', 'The towers…'. Use of bold and italics is up to you – but be consistent. You may use bold for any terms and italics for emphasis, for example.
2 *This is your chance to experiment on the computer. Does your work look clearer and easier to read than the original? If not, you may have made unnecessary alterations.*

Reading: story openings   Week 5 Tuesday

1(a) This line is very simple and short. It is an abrupt and slightly eerie start, as it introduces us to the idea right at the beginning, that nothing in Green Lake is as you would expect it to be. **(b)** The setting is hostile. We learn that the climate is hot and dry and the town and lake are said to have 'shrivelled and dried up'. The animals are not welcoming either – all are hostile and poisonous: rattlesnakes, scorpions and the yellow-spotted lizards. The atmosphere is still and threatening – like death. **(c)** The words 'usually' and 'always' add menace and emphasise a danger. They stand alone to underline the point they are making. 'Usually' alerts you to the possible danger and 'Always' repeats and heightens this fear. **(d)** We begin to see the Warden as a controlling and unkind person. We are told that the only shade – the hammock – is for the Warden only, and that 'the Warden owns the shade'.
2 *Make sure that you have followed the example in 'Holes'. Have you hinted at future events/dangers? Have you used language and punctuation to create an atmosphere? Have you played with sentence length?*

Punctuation: apostrophes and plurals   Week 5 Wednesday

1(a) You will – You'll **(b)** Will it not – Won't it **(c)** It does not – It doesn't **(d)** I cannot – I can't **(e)** I ought not – I oughtn't **(f)** I must not – I mustn't
2 horses, butterflies, witches, sheep, feet, clocks, women, buses

Writing: language choice   Week 5 Thursday

1 *Firstly, have you made the story sound exciting and dramatic? It is only your word-choice that can achieve this. Make sure that all 5 W questions may be answered: Who? What? Where? Why? When?*

Writing: to discuss   Week 5 Friday

1 *Make sure that your discussion is balanced – that you have discussed arguments for and those against equally. Check your use of paragraphs and that you have used logical connectives and phrases such as 'on the other hand'.*

Writing: building on descriptions   Week 6 Monday

1 inched/scurried/scuttled; cried/shrieked/barked; glanced/peered/gawped
2(a) The tow bar was broken meaning there was nothing to keep it away from her legs, so it kept slamming into her. **(b)** She starts by describing the sled as 'chasing' her. This begins the animal description. She describes it as if it had a mind of its own – 'an animal stalking me, waiting for my weak moments'. We really feel her frustration as she has lost all control and is having a battle with the sled, which is 'shimmying… jerking against the rope like a wild horse'.
3 *Make sure that the adjectives and verbs you have used bring your object to life – as in the example.*

Reading: understanding details   Week 6 Tuesday

1(a) Choose from: earthquakes, volcanoes, floods, droughts, storms, fires and landslides. **(b)** 1990 **(c)** True: **B, C (d)** Urban migrants are people who moved to the city to look for work. **(e)** Most of the article is fact. Opinion would be 'Something has to be done now.' **(f)** 'Urban concentration' means a high number of people living crowded together in towns and cities.

Writing: spelling strategies   Week 6 Wednesday

1 1 irresistible **2** all right **3** separate **4** harass **5** pursue **6** recommend **7** seize **8** cemetery **9** definitely **10** occasion **11** drunkenness **12** occurrence **13** weird **14** a lot **15** poem **16** embarrassment **17** repetition **18** accidentally **19** existence **20** privilege **21** immature **22** relative **23** illegal **24** incredible **25** accommodation **26** flexible **27** criticise **28** tomorrow **29** happiness **30** at all

Reading: understanding structure   Week 6 Thursday

1(a) The first paragraph sets the scene of the story (we know it is about a journey in the narrator's childhood), but it also makes the reader want to read on because it hints at 'dangers and ordeals' to come. **(b)**'Ill-fated' suggests that something went wrong, an exciting twist. **(c)** Virginia seems to have been a little nervous about making the journey, as she says: 'one of my main concerns was encountering Indians'. **(d)** 'Grandma Keyes had an aunt who had been taken prisoner by the Indians in an early settlement' – this makes the Indians seem threatening. '…so that no warrior could slip behind me with a tomahawk' – here, the Indians are portrayed as violent, and that they might sneak up when you are not expecting. '…all ready for the war dance' – this makes them seem ready for war and fighting. **(e)** Only **D** is actually specified in the text as true. **(f)** The final paragraph is particularly effective as it literally take us on a journey, away from the little horse. We are moving on with Virginia and are looking back at what she has left: the future is unknown. This makes the reader want to read on.

Punctuation: verbs, objects and tenses   Week 6 Friday

1(a) knew **(b)** the drums **(c)** Janie **(d)** the vet
2(a) will be **(b)** thought **(c)** like **(d)** grow up **(e)** grew up **(f)** ate
3 grew, held, ran, saw, brought, thought, sang, hung, took, read, made

Writing: to explain   Week 7 Monday

1 *Make sure that your response is sorted into logical paragraphs, which are linked using connectives. Suggested paragraphs: description of earth, rock and plates; mountain ranges, plates, earthquake areas; molten rock, volcano, lava.*

Reading: question types   Week 7 Tuesday

1(a) B (b) B (c) A (d) D

Writing: changing tenses   Week 7 Wednesday

1 *Your report must be in the present tense. The power of the volcano needs to be communicated through your choice of language. Is there a sense of occasion in the report? Is it exciting? Would it hold a viewer's interest? You can refer to yourself ('I') and address your viewers directly.*
2 *The same story will now be in the past tense. The language will be more formal, written in the third person/impersonal (no 'I') and must include Who? What? Where? Why? When?*

Reading: appreciating poems   Week 7 Thursday

1 *You should have noted any images/ideas that you thought of as you read the poem.*
2 The mood of the poem is nostalgic. Atwood is looking back on her childhood through the adult eyes she now has, there is also a tinge of sadness and regret: 'Why do I remember it as/sunnier all the time then…/I could hardly wait to get out of there…'
3 *Choose from:* holding the log for sawing; holding the string while he measured; weeding; sitting in the back of the car or in a boat.
4 Atwood means that she was paying close attention to all that her father did. She did nothing perhaps, but noticed every little detail. This is also a reflection of how the child sees everything 'close up' but is unable to see the bigger picture.
5 *Choose from:* 'greying bristles on the back of his neck'; 'Sometimes he would whistle'; 'He pointed such things out'; 'the whorled texture of his square finger, earth under the nail'.
6 Looking back on her childhood, Atwood 'would know' how precious it is – how the 'boring' things do not last forever, how her father will age and be separated from her and how she should savour every moment. Perhaps this is what she means by 'too much'.

Writing: homophones   Week 7 Friday

1 ascent; lightening; meddle; knight; oversees; bail; hoarse; grate; naval; paste
2 *The Prime Minister gave his assent (agreement); The mountaineers begun their ascent of Everest; The lightning struck the school; White paint has a lightening effect; The winner got a gold medal; Don't meddle in others' affairs; It is dark at night; He was her knight in shining armour; I want to travel overseas; The foreman oversees the builders on the site; Another bale of straw for the stable, please; The burglar was released on bail; The horse lives in the paddock; He shouted so much that he became hoarse; It was a great match; I like to grate my carrots; Your belly button is called your navel; He was a very respected naval officer; I paced up and down the room as I was so nervous; Flour and water together make a sticky paste.*

Reading: facts and opinions   Week 8 Monday

1(a) FACT **(b)** OPINION **(c)** FACT **(d)** OPINION **(e)** FACT
2 *Remember a fact is when the statement you make can be proven and is nothing to do with what someone thinks. An opinion is someone's own thoughts on the matter.*

Reading: advertisements   Week 8 Tuesday

1 *Make sure you have completed the table analysing a TV advert.*
2 *How effective is your advert? Be honest with yourself. What colours did you use and why? What images? Is there the right balance of copy and images? How did you make it appeal to your target audience?*

Reading: genre   Week 8 Wednesday

1(a) It is clear that this is an autobiographical text because it is written in the first person and the narrator is looking back over her life. **(b)** If it were a biography, it would be written by someone else and would be in the third person. It would be more formal in structure. *Suggested first line: Although Ms X has had a lengthy and successful career and a full and well-publicised private life, her glittering destiny grew from the humblest of beginnings.*
(c) *Suggested title: Blitz Baby*
2 *Make sure that the language you use works with the genre you have chosen.*

Writing: reviews   Week 8 Thursday
1 and 2 Check your review against the checklist on page 81. Make sure that you have used logical paragraphs and that your writing has the right tone and sounds professional.

Writing: common mistakes   Week 8 Friday
1 Choose which is the clearest handwriting and practise using it.
2 Be hard on yourself here. Use these answers, but judge for yourself as well. How could you improve your work?

Answers for Practice Reading Test

1 The demonstrators are smart and rich with big cars – not like typical demonstrators. They are middle class.
2 (a) *not a nose ring nor a wedge of braided hair in sight*
The writer's image of demonstrators is of young people with long hair and piercing.
(b) *sleek and comfortable*
The demonstrators are well off/very smart/rich looking/smug/confident.
3 The argument is that small communities have to play their part in providing energy/that NIMBY attitudes will mean more nuclear power or oil dependence.
4 If everybody takes the same attitude about protecting/saving their own area, the development of alternative energy will fail.
5 To make the article more real/contemporary/like news broadcast and to put forward/develop their views in more detail.
6 The writer is sarcastic/opposed to the demonstrators, sympathetic to the environmentalists and the ending suggests that he or she supports alternative energy sources.
7 Repetition of **pollutant**; mention of **culprits**; **acid rain**; **global warming**.
8 It starts with what people know, describes the stages in a process like a scientific explanation, uses **because**, and gives an example.
9 They focus on the negative features of traditional and nuclear fuels and then describe the positive features of hydrogen power. Hydrogen power is described as an ideal/jobs for all, clean factories, cheap clean power.
10 By making traditional fuels sound dirty and unattractive, then to make hydrogen power sound clean and inviting./By using a simple explanation of how it works./By using bullet points to underline the reasons why hydrogen power is better.
11 Clear headings separate the topics and break up the text, making it clearer and more interesting. Bullet points in the third section list the reasons clearly and can be referred to easily.
12 The long list emphasises the amount of rubbish that is thrown away.
It speeds up the text and almost seems to create the effect of a pile of rubbish. All the items just keep building up and up.
13 (i) burning **(ii)** burying
14 The questions are rhetorical. They bring the focus onto the reader and ask the reader direct questions to make him/her think and make the topic a personal one.
15 (i) poisonous **(ii)** unable to break down naturally – remain as litter forever
16 *Suggested summary: The article looks at the problem of waste disposal, especially given that, as a nation, we are producing more and more waste year upon year. It discusses alternatives to the traditional methods of disposal – burning and burying – focussing on the '3Rs', which are reduce, reuse and recycle.*

Answers for Practice Writing Test

Longer Writing Task

Check that you have:
- used adjectives to describe the waiting room;
- written about **two** people in separate paragraphs;
- used direct speech with a new line for each new speaker.

Shorter Writing Task

Check that you have:
- written in letter form;
- written more than one paragraph;
- used empathic language to show you feel sorry for Ben;
- set out what he could do differently.

Answers for Practice Shakespeare Test

Comment how: In the first scene they are arguing, duelling verbally. Beatrice says 'I wonder that you will still be talking...' and he calls her 'Lady Disdain'. In the second extract Benedick believes Beatrice loves him, so gone are the harsh words. He reads only love into her words, seeing 'double meaning'. Benedick believes Beatrice loves him, but her position has not changed, this weakens his position and provides comedy. You could also comment how in a sense, the change of heart is no surprise. Despite being the result of a trick, the pair are extremely well matched – their sparring in the first scene illustrates this. They are equals.

GUIDELINES FOR MARKING THE PRACTICE TEST

Reading
Marking your Practice Reading Test is straightforward. You can check your answers and work out your level using the table below.

Practice Reading Test marks	Reading Level
1-4	3
5-9	4
10-15	5
16-21	6
22-32	7

Writing
The Practice Writing and Shakespeare Tests are harder to assess. In the National Test, the examiner will look closely at your work and follow precise guidelines when allocating your marks. These guidelines can be found on the QCA website: http://www.qca.org.uk/45.html

Below you will find the level descriptors which will help you to assess your own writing and attribute it with a level. This can help you, not just in marking your Practice Tests, but in all of your writing.

Level	Description
3	Writing plain and unadventurous; spelling of simple words is accurate and sentences mostly contain capital letters and full-stops.
4	Writing is organised with more exciting words and sentence structures; commas and speech marks are mostly used correctly – full-stops and capital letters all of the time.
5	Writing suits the reader; spelling of longer and simple words is always accurate and some complex words are spelled correctly; reasonable paragraphs; more complex punctuation is normally accurate; quotation marks are used where necessary.
6	Shows some use of stylistic devices to suit both the reader and the purpose of the text; the reader's attention is held through a variety of sentence structures and types; writing is fluent and well-organised into logical paragraphs; spelling of most words is accurate.
7	Writing shows flair – well-developed, organised and coherent; paragraphs are logical and effective; a wide range of vocabulary is used and interesting effects are created; spelling of complex, irregular words is correct.

Shakespeare

Level	Description
3	Some understanding of the events and implications of the scenes, but no insight; attempts to support ideas with quotes, but not much; ideas are disjointed and do not hang together in an argument.
4	Simple ideas about how the relationship has changed, but too much emphasis on the characters and not enough comparison; some explanation of what is said, supported by some quotations, but these are not always relevant and are rather clumsily inserted into the answer; no attempt to draw ideas together and poor style makes them seem disjointed.
5	Greater understanding of the changes in the relationship, but still a tendency to focus on what the characters are generally like, rather than how they are shown in these scenes; there is no depth to the discussion as to how their relationship could be changing or why or what this may mean; style and structure is accurate but not very fluent.
6	More detailed examination of the language and what it shows about the characters; comment on the pair's suitability as well as their similarities in terms of pride and pigheadedness; some focus on the reasons for Benedick's change of heart and the ensuing comedy, although mention is brief; answer is clear, written in fluent paragraphs.
7	Clear development of all points with focussed analysis of the language in both scenes, what it shows and how; comments on the changes in the relationship, reasons and effect, as well as comment on their suitability, the irony and comedy of the scene; good knowledge of the play as a whole; answer is individual and shows flair in terms of analysis of the text and use of language.